Percival Lowell's Big Red Car

Percival Lowell's Big Red Car

The Tale of an Astronomer and a 1911 Stevens-Duryea

WILLIAM LOWELL PUTNAM

McFarland & Company, Inc., Publishers
Jefferson, North Carolina, and London

ALSO BY WILLIAM LOWELL PUTNAM

The Kaiser's Merchant Ships in World War I
(McFarland, 2001)

John Peter Zenger and the Fundamental Freedom
(McFarland, 1997)

Frontispiece: Percival Lowell, as envisaged in historical perspective by students of Flagstaff Junior High School — 1980 (Lowell Archives)

Library of Congress Cataloguing-in-Publication Data

Putnam, William Lowell.
Percival Lowell's big red car : the tale of an astronomer and a 1911 Stevens-Duryea / William Lowell Putnam.
p.   cm.
Includes index.

ISBN 0-7864-1234-8 (softcover : 50# alkaline paper)

1. Duryea automobile — History. 2. Lowell Observatory — Museums. 3. Lowell, Percival, 1855–1916 — Homes and haunts — Arizona — Flagstaff. I. Title.
TL215.D87P88   2002   629.222 — dc21   2002013025

British Library cataloguing data are available

©2002 William Lowell Putnam. All rights reserved

No part of this book may be reproduced or transmitted in any form or by any means, electronic or mechanical, including photocopying or recording, or by any information storage and retrieval system, without permission in writing from the publisher.

Front cover: Percival Lowell at the eyepiece of the
1896 24-inch Clark refractor *(Lowell Archives).*
Lowell's 1911 Stevens-Duryea at the Heiser ruins.
Back cover: Lowell's rendering of the planet Mars *(Art Today).*

Manufactured in the United States of America

*McFarland & Company, Inc., Publishers
Box 611, Jefferson, North Carolina 28640
www.mcfarlandpub.com*

Affectionately dedicated to the memory of
Warwick Eastwood,
keeper of the Stevens-Duryea Records

Contents

Preface	1
I. A Horseless Carriage?	7
II. The Earliest Automobiles	13
III. The Duryeas, Stevens and Automobile Manufacturing in Springfield	28
IV. The Stevens-Duryea	40
V. The Great Race	50
VI. The Brave New World of Automobiles	59
VII. The Motoring Lowells	72
VIII. Big Red's First Trip	84
IX. At Home in Flagstaff	98
X. Highways	119
XI. Big Red's Contemporaries	134
XII. Beyond Lowell's Death	141
XIII. Big Red Comes Home	162
Index	172

PREFACE

This is not the story of the American automobile industry — such a project would fill many shelves and in fact, already does. Rather, this book is written as the extended life story of but one vehicle, the product of America's first automobile maker, composed during the year of its ninetieth birthday, and while it was still in good health and capable of leading an active life.

Many of the peripheral figures in the evolution of the gasoline engine–powered automobile are mentioned, along with quite a number of the landmarks and leading figures of the subsequent automobile industry. But this narrative is focused on one car, the work of the younger of the once-famous Duryea brothers. It touches on the community in which they labored in short-lived teamwork, and the evolution of the automobile industry. With the subject vehicle's sale to Percival Lowell, whose horizon-opening astronomical theories, lectures and pronouncements made him a figure to this day of both controversy and prominence, the car went to the Arizona Territory and achieved a measure of its owner's reflected renown. That was only proper, for the auto he rode in was indisputably among the best — and still is.

This one vehicle became particularly noteworthy not only because it had one of the most distinguished owners in the land, but because it survived from 1911 when delivered to this owner, through his death in 1916, through further use to 1938 when it was "aban-

Preface

Percival Lowell in 1915, the year before his death (Lowell Archives).

doned," on through sixty years of absence and indolence, then rehabilitation, and finally to its return to Percival Lowell's Observatory on Mars Hill overlooking Flagstaff.

In this text, we touch on aspects of the evolution of the American machine tool industry, particularly as it pertained to automobile making, as well as the Duryea family and their competitive environment. The focus changes abruptly at the time when this one vehicle, Stevens-Duryea serial number 20700, made its debut in Flagstaff, then a frontier logging and cow town of Arizona with unpaved streets in what was not yet even one of the United States. Thereafter, we follow the tale of the venerable vehicle through its various owners to its present status as a moving landmark of history.

Any good public library contains dozens of books on the evolution of the automobile industry. Other than the lengthy expositions found in the *Encyclopædia Britannica*, three books were particularly helpful in illuminating the early industry in the United States: *The Treasury of Early American Automobiles—1877–1925* by Floyd Clymer (McGraw-Hill, 1925); *The American Automobile* by John B. Rae (University of Chicago Press, 1965); and David Burgess Wise's 1979 volume *The Illustrated Encyclopedia of the World's Automobiles*, published by A & W, New York. As a counter to these publications and with a more Eurocentric perspective, *The Star and the*

Preface

Laurel, the centennial history of Daimler, Mercedes and Benz, by Beverly Rae Kimes and published in 1986, was very informative.

This book deals heavily with the life and accomplishments of Lowells—particularly Percival, but with comments on the accomplishments of his siblings, as well. For further information on their lives, an essential source is *The Lowells and Their Seven Worlds* by Ferris Greenslet (Houghton, Mifflin; Boston, 1946). A different perspective on the Lowell family can be gained from Thomas H. O'Connor's *Lords of the Loom* (Scribners; New York, 1968). Boston's famous Lowell Institute was established by the will of John Lowell, Jr., in 1836 and furnished the pattern for the will of Percival that has guided and financed his Observatory. The Institute's history can be found in Edward Weeks's volume, *The Lowells and Their Institute* (Little, Brown; Boston, 1966). There are also a number of books on the Lowell Observatory, including a popular one by Rose Houk and a centennial piece by this author, *The Explorers of Mars Hill*, published in 1994.

Percival has excited more than one biography, starting with that written by his younger brother, Lawrence (Macmillan; New York, 1935). Another small, rare, and very touching volume was privately published in 1921 by Percival Lowell's more than admirable secretary, Wrexie Louise Leonard: *Percival Lowell, An Afterglow*. Most thorough, however, is a more recent biography by Professor David Strauss of Kalamazoo College: *Percival Lowell, The Culture and Science of a Boston Brahmin*, published in 2001 by Harvard University Press.

Lowell, this author's great-uncle, was a communicator, a prolific writer in addition to his popularity as a lecturer, authoring several volumes on Japan and the Far East before he directed his talents to astronomy. These books, completely incidental to the narrative that follows, are now rare items in their original language but remain in print to this day—in Japanese. His astronomical publications include: *Mars* (Longmans, Green; London, 1896); *The Solar System* (Houghton, Mifflin; Boston, 1903); *The Evolution of Worlds* (Macmillan; New York, 1909); *Mars as the Abode of Life* (Macmillan; New York, 1910); *Mars and Its Canals* (Macmillan; New York, 1911); and, of course his final work, the celebrated mathematical treatise on *A*

Preface

Trans-Neptunian Planet, published just before his death. Additional perspectives on the work of Percival Lowell can be gained from two volumes written by William Graves Hoyt and published by the University of Arizona Press: *Lowell and Mars* (1976), and *Planets X and Pluto* (1980). The scientific career of Lowell's most notable assistant, Andrew Ellicott Douglas, is well documented in George E. Webb's *Tree Rings and Telescopes* (1983, University of Arizona Press, Tucson). The travails of the talented Sykes brothers are very amusingly recounted in Godfrey Sykes's autobiographical work, *A Westerly Trend*, published in 1984 also by the University of Arizona Press.

Percival's younger siblings included, in order, Abbott Lawrence, born 1856; Katherine, born 1859; Elizabeth, born 1862; and finally Amy, born 1874, whose works as a poet and suffragette are still the subject of literary discussion. Katherine married twice (first to Alfred Roosevelt, after whose tragic death she married James Bowlker) and left numerous progeny. Elizabeth (Mrs. William Lowell Putnam, as she very firmly preferred to be known after her marriage) also wrote poetry — much of it held to be superior to that of Amy. The life of Lawrence, an authority on constitutional government whose impact on American higher education was vast, is well recorded in Henry Aaron Yeoman's 1948 volume *Abbott Lawrence Lowell (1856–1932)*, published by Harvard University Press.

Despite a number of detailed historical references pertinent to Flagstaff, this book is not intended to compete with the definitive and comprehensive history of that community compiled by a subsequent proprietor of Flagstaff's local newspaper, the *Arizona Sun*, Dr. Platt Cline. His volume, published in 1994, contains an introduction by one of the community's most notable citizens, the Honorable Bruce Babbitt, and is entitled *Mountain Town: Flagstaff's First Century*. The interested reader is directed to that exhaustive undertaking, and if its contents are in any way at variance with those of this book, it wins.

Other than those of the big red car itself, the numerous pictures of early automobiles that adorn this text were generously made available from the files of the Horseless Carriage Foundation of La Mesa, California, and the archives of Lowell Observatory. I would also like to thank the staff of the Connecticut Valley Historical Museum in

Preface

Springfield, Massachusetts, for their kind assistance. More recent photographs were taken by the author and Peter Rosenthal, without whose labors this undertaking would lack much of its character. Peter has, as in previous endeavors, also made many of the ancient photographs used herein clearer and better.

Besides those persons specifically mentioned in the text, such as Lowell Observatory's resident archive, Dr. Henry Lee Giclas, my thanks are many. Denise Colton, Mary Lou Evans, Ernesto Haase, Martin Hecht, Margaret Humberston, Robbert Leopold, Ian McNaught-Davis, the late Paul Sweitzer, James Watkins, and Roberta Watkins have all pitched in various tidbits. Meanwhile Kathryn, my wife and partner of half a century, has aided and abetted, normally quite graciously, with my attention to what all these kind people have supplied. At the end, however, if it hasn't all come together right, contact the undersigned.

William Lowell Putnam, III
Mars Hill, Flagstaff, Arizona

A Horseless Carriage?

After 1896, the Boston-born polymath Percival Lowell lived mostly in the southwestern frontier logging and cow town of Flagstaff, Arizona. Actually, the community was legally organized as a city of close to 2,000 souls, complete with mayor. But according to tradition, the American West had been won on horseback and most of its inhabitants still moved that way, so it was a significant leap of faith in 1910 just to try out one of those newfangled things that were beginning to appear in increasing numbers on the streets and roads of eastern America. To actually buy one, at a price of close to $6,000 (when a New York City subway ride cost only a nickel and the daily *Times* only one cent) and with a specially designed, extra-wide rear seat — that was a giant step. But Lowell, whose basic ideas about the presence of water, and even life, on the neighboring planet of Mars were proven right 85 years after his death, was nothing if he was not a futurist. For winter travel, he had used the first skis in the Arizona Territory — and thus one is inclined to wonder why it took him as long as it did to decide on purchase of an automobile.

The answer may lie in several factors. Fuel for these frequently scary devices was not readily available everywhere with the ubiquitousness to be found three generations later. This commodity was bought at the local grain and feed dealer in drums of various sizes. Lowell's observatory already had a sturdy barn, a wagon and two carriages, as well as the necessary horsepower to move them up to his

Percival Lowell's Big Red Car

Percival Lowell with Venus and some of her satellites — 1906 (Lowell Archives).

hilltop and wherever else he wished to go. Highways in the United States, particularly in the Southwest, were as scarce as the fuel needed for an internal combustion engine. Pavement was nonexistent. Besides, everyone knew how to drive a horse and carriage, while handling and especially caring for one of these noisy, unreliable and much more temperamental machines generally required the services of an expert. When the astronomer wanted to travel any great distance, one of the main transcontinental routes of the iron horse — the Santa Fe Railroad, with several passenger trains a day, east and west — ran right along the south boundary of his property. When he was staying nearer his ancestral roots in Boston, as he frequently did and where he later acquired a second (and second-hand) automobile, cabs and drivers were commonplace. It took a major and startling event, as will be seen below, to force the dramatic decision to buy such a machine.

I. A Horseless Carriage?

While today many thinking people on planet Earth have come to question the beauties and benefits of the gasoline engine, when compared with its incalculable physiological and environmental costs, modern astronomical science, and all that has flowed from it, owes a lot to Percival Lowell. He alone had the imagination to envisage and the courage to expound on the heretofore heretical topic of some form of life existing on distant celestial bodies. He, all but alone, had the faith to postulate the existence of more than a mere eight planets orbiting the sun, but was then completely alone in having the intellectual ability to prove it. He alone had the intestinal and financial fortitude to back the study at his observatory of distant nebulae which were then found to be receding from the Milky Way at frighteningly great speeds. The modern concept of an expanding universe was born on Mars Hill, where lived also Venus, the Observatory's cow, and Pegasus, Lowell's saddle horse, and where his garden grew prize watermelons.

Certainly a major factor in Lowell's decision to buy an automobile was the presence on his payroll of a man that Lowell knew could always fix it, if necessary make parts for it and be counted on whenever necessary to make anything work. Stanley Sykes was the younger of two brothers who had emigrated from London in 1886. Both Stanley and his brother, Godfrey, had been trained in mechanical arts at London's Finsbury Technical School, but the two brothers also had other talents. Godfrey, who also worked occasionally for Lowell but never became a permanent employee, turned out also to be an intriguing writer, and Stanley's paintings of the northern Arizona landscape show the talent he inherited from their father, who was a command artist to Queen Victoria.

When the brothers decided to leave England and settle in the wild American West, they bought their passage over the Atlantic and then continued toward their goal by working their way across the nation from New York, taking odd jobs along the way to enable their purchase of horses and provisions for the next few hundred miles. Reaching the locality called Turkey Tanks on the easterly outskirts of Flagstaff in the late fall of 1886, they took up some land and set out to become cattlemen. But the cattle business soon entered a depression and they were forced to fall back on their scholastic

Stanley Sykes (right) with E.C. Mills in his workshop on Mars Hill—1904 (Lowell Archives).

training. By 1892, they had completely relocated into town and set themselves up in business on Aspen Avenue as "Makers and Menders of Anything." In those days of non-motorized transport, their small machine shop's specialty soon became the fabrication and repair of bicycles. It was thus they were employed when Percival Lowell's advance man, 27-year-old Andrew Ellicott Douglass, came to town on April 3, 1884. After having tested the astronomical "seeing" at suitable high points near Tombstone, Tucson, Phoenix and Prescott, he needed some small repairs to his portable telescope and other equipment and was directed by friendly townsfolk to the Sykes brothers' machine shop.

    This event began a relationship for the 29-year-old Stanley that lasted until his death in 1955. After Douglass decided on a location at Flagstaff for Lowell's observatory, in 1896 Sykes became a permanent member of the Lowell staff and evolved into a confidant and

Percival Lowell with his bride, Constance Savage, in New York—1908 (Lowell Archives).

friend, not only to his first employer, but to two generations of successors in the management of Lowell's observatory. In addition, he transmogrified from a "Maker and Mender of Anything" into the foremost telescope machinist in the nation. The intricate parts that came from his precision workshop remain in reliable use a century after they were made and still show no signs of giving out.

If Percival Lowell lacked confidence in the care and repair of his newest purchase from a manufacturer (albeit America's first car maker) on the other side of the continent — as some of his subsequent correspondence indicated — he also knew that in the final analysis he had all the help he would ever need in Stanley Sykes. Thus the car he ordered came to town in the late summer of 1911.

The Stevens-Duryea Model "Y" touring car was and still is a spectacular sight. The big red car's wheels are set 58 inches apart and its front axle is spaced 142 inches from the rear. The car body itself is a full 76 inches wide and 193 inches front to rear. There were no bumpers in those days, so the initial points of impact were the front bushings of its leaf springs. Its massive, gas-fired headlamps, a foot in diameter, are 36 inches above the pavement and set 32 inches apart. The driver's seat is 47 inches above the roadway and the extra-wide rear seat is 55 inches across. The top of its windshield reaches 84 inches — the top of its canvas roof, however, rises another 6 inches higher. The six cylinders of its 40 horsepower engine are very distinguishable and extend cumulatively a total of 54 inches from the flywheel to the end of the crankcase. The reader is invited to go measure the comparable dimensions on a modern vehicle.

Stevens-Duryea called its color "mulberry red" and the list price for the standard Model "Y" "Big Six" was $4,300. The famous Percival Lowell was going to ride in a style befitting his self-image.

The Earliest Automobiles

The big red car was the product of a long and historic parentage in American ingenuity. It could be said that among its forebears was our nation's first president. While others made their mark elsewhere, the process of American invention was sparked by Alonso Phillips, a Springfield, Massachusetts, boy who developed the continent's first friction match in 1847. The people who actually made autos, however, came here from elsewhere — but they had a good reason to move to this area.

George Washington passed through Springfield, Massachusetts, on his way north from Virginia to take command of the colonial forces surrounding Boston in the autumn of 1776 and make a wider effort out of the Yankees' localized unrest. The following year, forcibly impressed with the need to have a reliable domestic source for the small arms required by his ragtag army, he selected that town, which had been settled in 1636, to be the site of the first arsenal of the United States—then unformed, but very much in need of weapons for its troops. His choice of this heretofore farming market center, with a population in those days of only 1,974, rather than any of several larger communities along the sea coast, was dictated by a very simple pragmatic necessity. Springfield was already an established regional hub for river and wagon-road transportation, but it lay a dozen miles upstream on the Connecticut River from a series of minor rapids that would be impassable for the omnipresent British warships. After the experience of losing Newport and then all of Narragansett Bay's Aquidneck Island to the Royal Marines, the new commander-in-chief was concerned that a similar force would surely be sent out to destroy such a vital arms manufactory if it were accessible from King George's command of the sea.

America's first president, therefore, unconsciously determined that Springfield would become a center of skilled metal-working and other allied trades. The nation's armory needed and attracted people able to produce the intricate parts and supply the desirable walnut stocks for muskets, and people with such abilities gravitated to the area. Before the end of the next century, the Springfield area was to be home to dozens of skilled labor-using companies that made products ranging from Hiram Maxim and Harold Wesson's famous guns to fine items for automobiles such as gauges and ignition systems.

Among those thus attracted to Springfield was Thomas Blanchard, the seventh child of Samuel and Susanna (Tenney) Blanchard, born in Oxford, in south central Massachusetts, on June 24, 1788, when Washington had been in office as president a bare 16 weeks. Tom's grandfather, also Thomas, had fought the British at Concord only a dozen years earlier. At the age of 13, as Horatio Nelson was destroying the Danish fleet off Copenhagen, young Tom was inventing an apple-paring machine. His first mechanical endeavor did much to establish the lad's credentials with the local housewives.

A few years later, at age 16, Tom went to live in nearby Millbury with an older brother who was in the business of making tacks from cut wire, slowly and by hand, hammering the head flat while holding the shank with tongs. Tom first came up with a device that counted the hourly piecework output of each of his brother's employees, and then rang a bell when he had completed his quota. Looking further ahead, Tom followed up with a machine that cut the wire and made the complete tack in one series of motions—and at a rate of five hundred per minute. While expediting tack production, the invention must surely have excited any latent Luddite* sentiment in

---

*So named from that of the legendary English workman, Ned Ludd, who, in 1779 organized the destruction of a number of labor-saving workplace devices. His example was emulated by many others during the depression years that followed the end of the Napoleonic Wars.

II. The Earliest Automobiles

Sutton. No matter; the machine worked well enough for Blanchard to sell the idea for the then enormous sum of $5,000, after which the prototype model stayed in service for more than twenty years.

Also in Sutton, on the banks of the Blackstone River, was a small gun factory owned by Asa Waters in which gun barrels were forged, welded and ground by hand, the traditional method. The proprietor had devised a system of performing the cruder elements of these functions by means of a water-powered trip-hammer. He followed this idea up with a primitive lathe device for turning the barrels to a uniform thickness but was unable to think up a means of cutting the metal for the irregular shape at the butt end of the weapon. Having heard of young Blanchard's tack-making machine, he called on the budding inventor to ask for his help. Tom suggested a concept which met with the older man's approval and then devised a heretofore untried cam action that quite readily solved the irregular shape problem. In some amazement, Waters than jokingly suggested that Blanchard was so clever that he might try coming up with a machine that could turn out the even more irregular shape of a wooden gun-stock.

Word of the young man's ability spread fast in the limited sphere of the gun trade and Blanchard was soon called to the United States Armory at Springfield to arrange similar turning motions in the metal-working machinery there—now the young nation's busiest arms producer. Before its days were over in the early 1960s, this armory was to equip American infantrymen in every conflict from the War of the Revolution through the Korean "Police Action." It became the home of the famous .30 '06, the "Springfield" rifle that was the standard weapon for military sharpshooters for the next fifty years, and it turned out more than nine million "Garand" semiautomatic M1 rifles during World War II.

In 1817, after one such consultation with the armory management, and while driving his carriage the long day's journey home to Millbury, the idea came to Blanchard for a lathe that really would turn out a thoroughly irregular shape—like a gun stock. Having some capital from the sale of rights to his tack-making machine, Blanchard retreated to his laboratory workshop and commenced to fabricate his unique lathe. Two years later he presented Asa Waters with a miniature working model. The private gun maker promptly ordered a full-sized machine.

Pride in his latest invention inspired Blanchard to inform others and offer the idea to his nation's government. On November 18, 1818, with Indian wars still bothersome in Florida and the Midwest, he once again received a letter from Colonel Rosewell Lee (1777–1833), a native of Canaan, New York, who came to the Springfield Armory after the War of 1812 and remained its commandant for 16 years after 1815: "Sir: I wish to employ you immediately for the purpose of putting in motion a draw-grinding machine and perhaps one for turning barrels. Please inform me when you will be here and what materials will be necessary for the machine and dimensions."

Blanchard reported as requested and soon thereafter carried his miniature model lathe to Washington. It was said that while showing his device to the military and naval "brass," one officer asked if the machine was capable of adaptation to turning out a 74-gun frigate. To this the inventor is alleged to have replied, "Yes, sir; if you will furnish the block." Such joking aside, the Blanchard lathe was promptly purchased for use at the Springfield Armory. However, there must be some error in this anecdote. A frigate was the wind-powered cruiser of its day, carrying between 24 and 50 guns; the larger "ship-of-the-line" carried up to and often more than 80 guns. Horatio Nelson's flagship, HMS *Victory*, carried 100 guns and displaced 2,162 tons of water. The United States Navy had a lot of frigates and other men-of-war but never had any ships of the line comparable to those of other powers until they began to be made of steel. In any case, within a few years and before a variety of other potential users grasped its utility, the inventor was applying his concept to the turning of shoe lasts, statuary, oxbows and countless other irregular shapes.*

Blanchard nevertheless had a great deal of difficulty protecting his patent rights to this novel idea and was forced not only to defend his priority of invention in a dozen lawsuits but to implore the Congress to grant him a special extension of exclusivity on his mechanical breakthrough because of the government's own infringements

---

*A woodcut print of Blanchard's lathe can be found in Hezekiah Butterworth's Growth of Industrial Art.

II. The Earliest Automobiles

during his initial period of development. In the meantime he had taken up residence in Springfield so he could live in proximity to his major employer.

The inventor's talents, however, were not fully taken up with work at the Armory up on the hill. In Springfield's local weekly newspaper, the *Republican*, of Wednesday, November 22, 1826, a generation before Samuel Bowles's periodical had become a daily paper and begun to achieve its national status, the citizens of Springfield, Massachusetts, read the following column:

MR. BLANCHARD'S STEAM CARRIAGE

This ingenious piece of mechanism was exhibited here publicly for the first time last week. A short description of it will undoubtedly be acceptable.

On the hind axle, between the wheels, is placed a bevel-geared wheel, running parallel with the carriage wheels. On this bevel wheel there are two circles of cogs: the outer or largest circle is nigh its periphery; the other about halfway between the former and the axletree. To the axletree is attached in a horizontal position, a spindle or arbor, at such a distance from the bevel-geared wheel as to admit of two small pinion wheels, to ply into, or take hold of, the circles of cogs. These pinion wheels revolve freely on the spindle: and either of them can be coupled at pleasure to its corresponding circle of cogs, to give the carriage a forward motion. This is affected in the following manner: a coupling box, with level attached, is made fast to the spindle betwixt the pinion wheels; by means of the lever, the steersman can give the carriage any degree of speed, according to the level, or the ascent of the inclined plane. For instance, in ascending an inclined plane, the steersman, by moving the lever, couples the pinion wheel which meshes into the outer circle of cogs, thus giving the greatest extent of leverage, and affording a slow and strong motion. By using the lever again and coupling the inner pinion to the smaller circle of cogs, the motion of the carriage is accelerated, while the velocity and application of the power of the engine remain the same as in the other operation.

Instead of having its direction controlled with reins to the lead horses as all prior vehicles had been guided, Blanchard's carriage was steered by a device somewhat akin to the tiller of a sailboat, as were almost all subsequent horseless vehicles until 1902. Contemporary observers noted that "the steersman" operated a rod, inserted into the "forward axletree" by means of which the carriage could be "readily carried backward or forward and turned in any direction."

Blanchard's objective was to test the practicality of a vehicle that could operate on land using no expensive iron-shod roadbed as was required for the steam locomotives then coming into use in England. The *Republican*'s reporter noted that the invention had been duly patented but that Blanchard intended to bring out a new and more highly powered model "to be in readiness at the opening of the spring." Unfortunately, no further reports were forthcoming. In England, however, development of steam-powered carriages proceeded apace.

Blanchard did not invent the steam engine, nor was he the first to apply its motive power to motion on wheels. The former honor is generally credited to the Englishman Thomas Newcomen in 1712, and the latter in 1769 to the Frenchman Nicholas Cugnot. But Blanchard's recognition of the importance of shifting the engine's output to higher (or lower) speeds was important, and his construction of a differential gear was a truly notable breakthrough for his successors. Crudely described in the *Republican*'s article, the latter was the essential device for safe propulsion and dirigibility of all subsequent non-tracked motive power.

Flanged railroad wheels are rigidly affixed to their axles and the whole turns as a unit, the adjustment to curvature being made by the often unnoticed conical bevel of the wheels themselves which the motion of the vehicle throws to the outside of every curve, thereby increasing the diameter of the outer wheels to make them travel a greater distance with each revolution, while decreasing that of the inner. This process being impossible for non-flanged wheels or on roadways, Blanchard's invention of the differential gear in 1826 was fundamental to modern travel. Largely unrecognized at the time, it had long since passed into the public domain by the time others brought out a superior "horseless carriage" with a more highly evolved form of internal motive power. Blanchard is not often given credit for this device, though he used it in practice a full year before the French inventor Onésiphore Pecqueur independently devised the same concept for application to other as yet unbuilt motorized wagons.

There are always cynics however, and Blanchard's ideas provoked their share, for a less reverent but anonymous and a much later

II. The Earliest Automobiles

observer subsequently noted in the *Springfield Shopping News* of November 8, 1933:

> It was a crude steam engine, resting on a platform mounted on wheels. When he was ready for his trial trip, Blanchard announced that he proposed to run his new fangled wagon from his home on Main Street, just below Wilcox, [north] up Main Street to Carew and return to his home. [This is a total distance of less than three miles.] He started up at 8 o'clock in the morning but he had trouble with his engine before he had gone very far and the car stalled. His fire then went out and he had to get steam up again. But Blanchard was undaunted and finally made the trip to Carew Street and back, reaching his home at 4 o'clock in the afternoon, having propelled his car the entire distance with steam power.

It was to be 67 years before the Duryea brothers, Charles and Frank, propelled America's first internal-combustion powered vehicle along some of the same streets of Springfield.

While horses had already been successfully replaced in the 16th century by two-masted wagons using sail-power in the Netherlands, Blanchard's use of steam power for a trackless vehicle came long before the internal combustion engine was invented. But it was followed up some seventy years later by two other Yankees, Francis Stanley and his brother, Freelan (about whom more below). But Blanchard was on a smart track; his carriage weighed about a thousand pounds, complete with its two-inch bore, eleven-inch stroke engine, and was able to carry a payload of about its own weight up "any reasonable degree of ascent" as well as be controllable "in every way" when going down.

Blanchard's curiosity on the use of steam power for land propulsion having been satisfied, the inventor then turned to its use on water. In all he built four boats for use on the Connecticut River above and below Springfield and then several more for use on the Ohio River below Pittsburgh. Along the way Blanchard was among the first to recognize that rigidly mounted paddles, as were then applied to both side and stern-wheel driven boats, though simple to install, did not deliver the most efficient propulsive force from the power applied. During only a small part of the time spent submerged was any one paddle blade moving water directly astern; if the wheel were mounted half its radius above water level, the initial movement of each stroke tended to push water downwards as much as to the rear, and as the blade was rising at the end of its immersion, almost as much effort was then being put into lifting water as into moving the boat.

One way to correct this obvious inefficiency required that the paddle wheel itself be mounted so high as to barely skim the surface of the water, at best a risky condition if there were any wave action. Making use of his expertise on the applications of cams, Blanchard's latest device rotated on the same axle as the wheel itself and, by means of a second connecting rod, pitched each of the blades in turn so they would enter the water at exactly a right angle to the water surface, and retain that angle until they were lifted clear by rotation of the wheel. Blades could thus be set much deeper and drive the ship a great deal more effectively. This was not an easy device to envisage, nor was it always subsequently applied after its invention, but one concept Blanchard clearly understood was the effective operation of cams. Use of such a blade-adjusting system greatly increases the efficiency of the paddle wheel as a driving device.* In later years, Blanchard migrated to Boston and continued to invent practical devices ranging from "knees" for ships' timbers to hand-held (and fracture resistant) slates for school children, until his death in 1864.

The evolution of the "modern" automobile did not begin with Thomas Blanchard, nor even the brothers Duryea. It appears to have started in France in 1767, when Nicholas Cugnot applied steam power to a three-wheeled vehicle with the idea of using this motive device to haul King Louis XV's artillery. After a few years of development, his machine ran — but not very well. Its single front wheel, which did both the driving and the directing, was very heavily weighted with its steam boiler being placed ahead of the wheel. Thus, while the device could make up to three miles per hour, it was almost impossible to steer. Greater success was achieved in England where the 32-year-old Richard Trevithick, fresh from saving the Cornish tin mines by his use of steam-powered pumps, built a steam-powered carriage in 1803

---

*See Biographical Sketch of Thomas Blanchard and His Inventions, by Asa H. Waters, Worcester, 1878. This efficiency enhancing device is extremely well displayed at the Royal Observatory Museum in Greenwich.

II. The Earliest Automobiles

which made up to nine miles an hour on the streets of London. Though it was unpopular in some circles because it tended to scatter pedestrians and horses in all directions, others nevertheless followed.

The use of the internal combustion (for many years called the "explosion") engine, however, began in 1860 when a French patent was issued to a 38-year-old Belgian Jesuit priest, Jean/Joseph Etienne Lenoir. He used coal gas as a fuel and his device was sufficiently effective that he made and sold more than a hundred machines over the next few years. Two years after Lenoir, Frenchman Alphonse Beau de Rochas took out a patent on a four-cycle engine, but he seems never to have built one. Lenoir, however, actually ran his internal combustion–powered vehicle from the center of Paris to Joinville le Pont in 1862—a distance of only ten kilometers—in slightly more than two hours' time. (In a sign of what was to come, it took about the same length of time for this author to make the same trip by a modern car 138 years later.) But Lenoir's demonstration drive was a "first" and was sufficiently impressive that the liberal-thinking Czar Alexander II of Russia bought the prototype machine and took it home to St. Petersburg. The Duryea brothers of Springfield used an engine on the pattern of the German inventor, Nikolaus Otto, who had borrowed heavily from the work of Lenoir.

By 1865, the horse breeders and their political allies, the railroads, had begun to strike back. In London, Parliament passed a law that required any steam-powered vehicle on the public ways of Great Britain to go no faster than four miles per hour and be preceded by a man on foot carrying a red flag. Extended to other types of engines, this remained the law of that land until 1896, and similar laws were enacted in other countries and several of the United States. Back on the continent, in 1876 Nikolaus Otto (1832–1891) now devised a four-cycle gasoline engine that was a cumbersome two meters high, but sufficiently effective that he was soon hired by the 34-year-old Karl Benz and later the 55-year-old Gottfried Daimler, who brought out their first motor vehicles in 1885. Meantime, in 1880 in the Austrian capital of Vienna, 50-year-old Siegfried Markus had spent several years toying with an internal-combustion engine and vehicle that was too ugly to suit his neighbors and the very sight of which scared their horses. To assuage their fears he took his vehicle out of its garage only at night, but it then proved to be too noisy and was banned completely from the city's streets.

Across the Atlantic in 1873, English-born George Bailey Brayton made a two-cycle-engine-powered vehicle that was used on the streets of Providence, demonstrated at the Philadelphia Centennial Exhibition in 1876 and featured later that year by Phineas Taylor Barnum. Brayton is elusive in most biographical references, but in a further sign of things to come, his distant cousin Charles Ray Brayton (1840–1910) was the first chief of the Rhode Island State Police. Before he assumed his office (behind a billboard, presumably) things began to pick up speed and the American automotive industry took on some of the entrepreneurial aspects of the computer manufacture and software industries of a century later — many entries, but few survivors. Basically, the wheel, bicycle and wagon makers evolved into auto makers. The venerable firm organized in Buffalo in 1865 by George Pierce underwent an even longer metamorphosis, from bird cage maker to spoke maker for bicycle wheels to wheel-maker for bicycles to bicycle maker to motorized bicycle maker to automobile manufacturer. Before the industry stabilized it seemed that almost everyone had tried for a piece of the action. Notable landmarks in the field of transportation over the next generation included the following:

1875 • Daimler produces 634 two-stroke gasoline engines with an aggregate horsepower of 735.
1876 • 42-year-old Nicholas Otto produces his first four-stroke engine.
  • Philadelphia Centennial exposition shows five Daimler-built engines in "Machinery Hall."
1877 • Thomas Alva Edison demonstrates his phonograph.
1878 • Karl Benz demonstrates a motorized tricycle that attains a speed of seven miles per hour.
1879 • George Baldwin Selden, a 33-year-old American patent attorney, files Application #549,160, in his own name, based on the engine developed by Brayton.
1880 • Baku oil fields are developed by the Rothschilds and Alfred Nobel.

II. The Earliest Automobiles

- New York City streets are lit by electricity.
- Speed of light measured by A. A. Michelson; receives Nobel prize in 1907.

1881
- St. Gotthard tunnel opened after nine years of work.

1882
- Edison designs first hydroelectric plant for Appleton, Wisconsin.

1883
- Brooklyn Bridge opens for traffic.
- Hiram Maxim's machine gun fires ten shots per second.

1884
- Sir Charles Parsons devises a steam turbine engine.
- Standard Time adopted at an international conference in Washington.

1885
- Gottfried Daimler develops carburetor to maintain continuous fuel supply for engines.
- Armand Peugeot begins by selling Daimler's cars in France for Emile Levassor.
- Benz makes his first single-cylinder automobile engine; patented next year.

1886
- Gottfried Daimler builds his first automobile, producing 1.5 horsepower.
- On 3 July, Benz test drives his automobile around Mannheim.
- Severn River Tunnel opens.
- Bartoldi's Statue of Liberty is presented to the United States.

1887
- Alfred Krupp dies at age seventy-five.
- Emile Levassor goes into business with René Panhard.

1888
- Dr. John Boyd Dunlop, a prosperous 49-year-old Scots veterinarian, invents the pneumatic tire; franchises are soon granted worldwide.
- Heinrich Hertz discovers electromagnetic waves, a precursor to radar.

1889
- Leon Serpollet of France devises the "flash" boiler, enabling smaller steam engines to attain usable power in two minutes. First such models are made to order by Armand Peugeot.

- The Duryea brothers read an article in *Scientific American* about the work of Karl Benz.
1890
- Charles Hermann Steinway, piano maker of New York, bankrolls his son, William, in importing Daimler's cars to America.
1891
- Levassor and Panhard develop a new style of vehicle with the engine forward of the driver.
- Construction begins on the Trans-Siberian railroad; completed in 1905.
1892
- On 19 April, Charles and Frank Duryea bench test their first model.
- Rudolph Diesel patents his version of an internal combustion engine.
1893
- A Bureau of Road Inquiry is established within the U.S. Department of Agriculture.
- Benz "Victoria" develops 5 HP; burns 1 liter of gasoline per five Km and exceeds 35 KPH.
- On 8 September, Frank Duryea drives around Springfield in the brothers' second motor vehicle (now in the Smithsonian Institution).
1894
- Elwood Haynes builds a one-cylinder car in Kokomo for the Apperson Brothers, wagon makers.
- First two-cylinder automobile engine built by Duryea brothers.
- World's first automobile race won by a car with a Daimler engine.
1895
- Selden's patent is granted; he begins issuing licenses and extracting royalty payments.
- Haynes gets the world's first traffic ticket, being ordered off the streets of Chicago by a policeman who caught up with him on a bicycle.
- Hiram Percy Maxim, son of the expatriate gun-maker, becomes chief engineer of Albert Augustus Pope's Electric

II. The Earliest Automobiles

Vehicle Company of Hartford, CT; company declared bankrupt in 1907.
- On 11 July, Emile Levassor leads a 21-car field in driving 1,200 kilometers of the straight, tree-lined Route Nationale from Paris to Bordeaux in less than 49 hours, averaging 14.9 MPH.
- 28 November, Frank Duryea wins America's first auto race, sponsored by the Chicago *Times/Herald;* goes 55 miles (89 km) in the rain and snow at an average speed of 7 MPH.

1896
- On 6 March, Charles Brady King drives his first car down Detroit's Woodward Avenue.
- On 2 April, the second model of the Duryea automobile is exhibited by Barnum & Bailey.
- On 4 June, Henry Ford drives his first car down Bagley Avenue in Detroit.
- 14 November, two Duryea cars lead the pack in a race from London to Brighton.

1897
- In April, Levassor dies while working at his drawing board; Daimler's daughter is named Emilie.
- On 19 October, George Mortimer Pullman dies.
- Benz finishes making his 381st "Velo."

1898
- Paris Metro opens.
- Graf Ferdinand Zeppelin builds his first motor-driven airship.

1899
- Ransom Olds is backed by a mining magnate, Samuel Smith, who puts up $199,000 for 95 percent of the company's stock. Six hundred "Merry Oldsmobiles" are subsequently made in 1901, 2,500 in 1902, 4,000 in 1903 and 5,000 in 1905;
- Automobiles are banned from New York's Central Park.
- Automobiles are taxed in Columbus, Ohio, for road upkeep.
- First auto shows are held in Chicago and New York.
- Daimler delivers 6 HP staff car to German War Ministry.
- A total of 3,723 cars are made in America.

Percival Lowell's Big Red Car

1900 • First horseless fire engines are made.

- Republican party adopts a "Good Roads" plank in its national platform.
- 23-year-old Louis Renault builds and sells 350 automobiles; France leads the world in per capita ownership of automobiles.
- 4,192 motor vehicles are made in America, selling for an average price of a little more than $1,000.
- After ten years of making tires, André and Edouard Michelin bring out their first guidebook for motorists.

1901 • Knox, Ford and Franklin cars appear.

- Wilhelm Maybach builds the first car made for Mercedes, daughter of Austro-Hungarian politician and magnate Emil Jelinek.
- Henry Ford defies Selden and litigates his patent rights; Selden is upheld, but other car makers are deemed not to have infringed. Ford becomes a folk hero.
- Edward Phelps Allis merges his company with that of William James Chalmers.

1902 • American Automobile Association founded.

- Pierce-Arrow cars appear.
- Benz two-seat "Spider" reaches 60 KPH and costs 8,500 gold marks.
- The steering knuckle is invented, enabling the front wheels to be turned by a wheel rather than a tiller; automobiles become much more steerable.

1903 • Cadillac, Hudson and Peerless cars appear.

- Barney Oldfield makes better than a mile a minute speed over a ten-mile course.
- American auto exports exceed $1.2 million.

II. The Earliest Automobiles

- Three vehicles cross the continent of North America from New York to San Francisco.*
- Parliament establishes a new British speed limit of 20 MPH.

1904
- Maxwell, Marmon and Reo cars appear.
- First Vanderbilt cup race won by average speed of 52.2 MPH.
- American car makers produce 21,692 vehicles.
- Charles Jasper Glidden organizes his first automobile tour.
- Motor busses ordered for London; delivery next year.

1905
- "Typhoid Mary" Mallon taken to isolation home in New York City's first motorized "paddy wagon."

In the calendar year of 1909 American car makers produced a total of 126,593 vehicles and the rush was in full flood. Five years later the total was close to half a million. Even Detroit's 65-year-old bachelor merchant prince, Joseph Lowthian Hudson, got his name on an automobile simply by bankrolling the ideas of Roy Chapin and Howard Coffin. Before the great shake-outs of the 1920s, there would be almost three thousand different marques made and sold in America by more than 1,500 different manufacturers, most of whom were basically assemblers of components made by various subcontractors.

Along with a very respectable number of important developments in automotive engineering and feats of driving these machines, the French managed another distinction. The per capita record for number of automobile marques—as well as that very word itself—clearly belongs in that nation. The varied and changing combinations of names reflected in the panoply of French automobiles may well be explained as another manifestation of the never-ending Gallic propensity to disagree over basically unimportant details and insist upon doing things differently.

---

*The first of these adventurous journeys was done to prove a $50 bet. The cross-country trip by Dr. Nelson Jackson, of Burlington, Vermont, and his chauffeur, Sewall Crocker, took two months. However, Jackson was fined en route for exceeding a local 6 MPH speed limit!

THE DURYEAS, STEVENS AND AUTOMOBILE MANUFACTURING IN SPRINGFIELD

> *Even as Charles and Frank Duryea were enjoying their first successes with horseless carriages, the brothers had a bitter argument — apparently over whether to build big cars or small — and it was the end of the Duryea Motor Wagon Company. The older brother, Charles, soon went back nearer his Midwestern roots and made low-cost, three-cylinder cars for many years. Frank stayed in Springfield and evolved a much larger business with the help of Joshua Stevens. Until the business was acquired by the heirs of George Westinghouse in 1918, they made some of the proudest luxury cars in the world.*

Charles Edgar Duryea was born in 1863, the eldest of the five children of George and Louisa Duryea. His brother, James Frank, came along eight years later, after the family had moved some forty miles northeastward from near the city of Canton, in Fulton County southwest of Peoria, to the smaller hamlet of Washburn, Illinois. In the years to come, Frank became party to more and bigger motor vehicles than his older brother, but all historians of automotive matters agree that Charles was the initial inventive genius and deserves credit as the principal figure behind the evolution of America's first

III. The Duryeas, Stevens and Automobile Manufacturing

usable automobile, though Frank was clearly the one whose labors gave the Duryea name its greatest prominence. But the name already had a long and interesting history.

As the long and tumultuous reign (1642–1715) of "Sun King" Louis XIV of France progressed, it became ever more obvious that his distrust of the "wrong thinking" Protestant Huguenot citizens of his country was going to have serious consequences—most likely for them. By 1685, forty-three years into his reign, when he finally revoked his grandfather Henri IV's 1598 Edict of Nantes, which guaranteed freedom of worship for all Frenchmen, many nonconformists had already quietly left, taking with them a great deal of their nation's ferment and inventiveness. Among those exercising this drastic option was Joost Durje, who initially took up residence at Mannheim, Germany, then the seat of the Rhine Palatinate. His non–Gallic family name had originated in Fifeshire on the east coast of Scotland several centuries earlier and crossed to France during the centuries when the French and the Scots were frequently allies against the common English enemy between them.

The fallout from Europe's Thirty Years War of religion, which devastated central Germany, continued to offer Durje little emotional solace, so in 1675, he and his wife, neé Magdalena LeFebre, set out on a longer trip, crossing the Atlantic to settle in the English-speaking, but Protestant-managed, Colony of New York. There, at Blissville on Long Island, he prospered as a potato farmer for fifty years, until his death in 1727. The line of descent from Joost and Magdalena's offspring to the famous automotive brothers, six generations later, was as follows:

Charles Duryea	m	Marie Robinson
Charles Duryea	m	Antie Guyn
John Wesley Duryea	m	Margaret Ann Welsh
Wesley Duryea	m	Elizabeth Byram
George Washington Duryea	m	Louisa Melvina Turner

After attending local schools near Washburn, northeast of Peoria, Charles Edgar Duryea finished his formal education with residence at Gitting's Academy in La Harpe, some hundred miles to the west. His graduation thesis in 1878 bore the prophetic title of "Rapid Transit Other Than on Rails." In this document, inter alia, he predicted the evolution of flying machines that would enable people to cross the Atlantic Ocean to Europe in half a day.

Following graduation, Charles went on to devise enhancements to the now omnipresent bicycle — one of which he had already fabricated several years earlier back on the farm, from broken and disused parts of agricultural implements. This device is not to be confused with its partial ancestor, the velocipede, which was usable only by the extremely agile because of its high front wheel, which made mounting and getting into motion a difficult procedure. Among the Duryea improvements to the bicycle — in that day of mediocre roads — was a coiled spring element in the front of the frame that took some of the uncomfortable bounce out of ruts and gravel. The quick and ubiquitous spread of the pneumatic tire, however, soon made this device unnecessary for lower speed bicycles, though it has continued in use elsewhere and is popular in modern trail bikes. Charles then came up with the "drop frame," a concept which enabled skirted ladies to ride a bicycle more decorously. This more long-lived and widespread idea was patented on January 5, 1886.

When the brothers received some funding for implementing what they had read about the gasoline-fueled "explosion" engine device pioneered by Karl Benz, they moved their base of operations to Springfield — then home to the nation's largest supply of skilled machinists as well as their first "angel." There, in a loft on Worthington Street, they labored on their horseless carriage. This "laboratory" was located only two blocks south of the railroad station and not much farther east of the Connecticut River, both of which afforded means of transportation their work was destined to largely supplant. By 1895 they had improved on their first horseless carriages, incorporating Dr. Dunlop's pneumatic tires and building a four-cycle, water-cooled engine with clutch and geared transmission that featured three forward speeds and one in reverse.

In February of the following year, the Duryea Motor Wagon Company offered its first car for sale and then made twelve more before the year was out. Leaving their business in the hands of their associates, the brothers took time off in November to accompany two

III. The Duryeas, Stevens and Automobile Manufacturing

of their vehicles being shipped to Europe. On the 14th, both Duryea automobiles came in seventy minutes ahead of all the other entries in a 52-mile race from London to the summer resort of Brighton on England's south coast. That nation's "red flag" law was definitely a thing of the past.

But disagreements surfaced between the two pioneers, the exact nature of which has been debated and analyzed by numerous subsequent commentators—but never conclusively settled. Certain facts are on the public record: Charles never took up legal residence in the city where he made his first automobile, but Frank maintained his legal domicile in Springfield until his retirement from the automotive business in 1915. When the famous Chicago race occurred (see below) in 1895, Charles was among those attending, but all accounts noted him as being a visiting spectator from Peoria. Based on the ways they each took when separated, it would seem likely that their very success led to the divisive decision which segment of the evolving automobile market they should pursue—the high end, or the low. By 1897 both of them had left the Duryea Motor Wagon Company, which soon folded its doors. Frank continued in business with his remaining associates, some distance removed from their original loft on Worthington Street. By 1902, though continuing to reside in Springfield, he was listed as being manager of an auto factory in Chicopee Falls and after 1905, its vice president. The inventive genius and skill which each brother had brought to the enterprise had dissolved in the bitterness, recriminations and self-justifications which only a family dispute can engender. Several publications ensued, wherein each brother decried the part played by the other. Even in their obituaries there was disagreement (See Appendix A) as to the facts of primacy in their work.

Charles went back first to Peoria, where he made a number of cars over the next three years. Then he migrated east to near Reading, Pennsylvania, where he organized the Duryea Power Company and made several hundred three-cylinder and three-wheeled motor vehicles, largely along one of the patterns used in Springfield, over the next sixteen years. He had married Rachel Steer in 1884 and had three children, Rhea Edna, Grace Louise and Merle Junius. Charles became a widely quoted authority and historian of the automobile, publishing the *Handbook of the Automobile* in 1906 and *The Automobile Book* in 1916. He died, surrounded by his devoted family, at his home in Philadelphia, of heart ailments on September 28, 1938.

On the next day a lengthy obituary appeared in the *New York Times*, followed on Friday, September 30, by an unusual editorial reading in part as follows:

> Charles Duryea never claimed to be the inventor of the first gasoline automobile. Nor does the Smithsonian Institution, where his earliest commercial car is preserved, pretend that he was. He was a synthesizer who had the rare mechanical wit to see how the contributions of his predecessors could be combined into a sound invention.... Why did Duryea die poor? Like so many inventors, he was unable to overcome the inertia of his own mind and adapt himself to public taste.... Duryea persisted in mounting the engine at the rear of the body and continued to provide a handle or tiller for steering and controlling the speed. His keener rivals saw the trend more clearly than he and snatched commercial supremacy from him. It is the old story of inventive ability without business sense, yet a heartening story too.... Here was an obscure Yankee mechanic who laid the foundations of a major industry and who might have dominated it had he possessed the flexibility of mind and the organizing gift that the exploitation of a great invention demands.

J. Frank (he almost always used the first initial only) stayed in the Springfield area, where he soon found yet another "angel" in the form of the business heirs of a well-to-do but now retired gun-maker. Joshua Stevens (1814–1906) was born during the final days of the ill-begotten War of 1812, which was disparagingly referred to in New England as "Mr. Madison's War" and generated a great deal of secessionist sentiment in the region. He was educated in the Berkshire hill town of Chester, 25 miles by wagon road west-northwest of Springfield. Though not of *Mayflower* ancestry, Stevens very much qualified as a Yankee, his forebears having been millers and farmers for several generations and active in the settlement of New England by the white-skinned invaders that flowed unstoppably into the region after 1630. By 1828, Joshua, Jr. had completed his three-year apprenticeship in a local machine shop and left the hardscrabble hill town for the big city down in the valley. Springfield's population had now

III. The Duryeas, Stevens and Automobile Manufacturing

graduated into five digits and the region was the center of the nation's small arms industry, while heavier, artillery weapons were now being made at the easterly end of the state in the Watertown Arsenal.

The hill-country teenager found employment over the next several years with a number of gun-makers, most notably Samuel Colt, who had given up the study of astronomy for the more practical trade with which his name was thereafter associated. Employed by other gun-makers during most of the Civil War years, Stevens finally took his designs to a small two-story building in Chicopee in 1864, where he made single shot .22 pocket pistols for several years in partnership with W.B. Fay and Amos Bartlett. Several lines of small-bore sport rifles were brought out over the next twenty years before the enterprise was reconstituted as the J. Stevens Arms & Tool Co. The latter word lay behind the firm's fabrication of calipers and other "fine" instruments that could readily be turned out on the same machine tools as precision firearms.

Stevens, who had been a vigorous abolitionist, a supporter of John Brown, and a staunch Republican, withdrew from the business in 1896 at age 82, and it was his successors in the management that made the most of the opportunity brought to their doorstep by the 30-year-old Frank Duryea with his ideas about — and proven successes with — horseless carriages. The Stevens Arms Company was to continue in business at 9 Montgomery Street in Chicopee Falls long after Stevens-Duryea automobiles ceased to be made until it was finally absorbed into the Savage Arms Company in the decades after World War II.

In Chicopee at that time was one Albert Henry Overman, also a native of Fulton County, Illinois, whose father had been one of the major tree nursery growers of the state. Educated at the state normal school, in 1870 he moved to Chicago. After the usual tentative feelers into other occupations, Overman, now in his mid-twenties, migrated east to Hartford where he developed plans for a bicycle-making business — starting with the making of the necessary wheels. Unable to find an appropriate location in Hartford, he relocated north to Chicopee Falls, and found space not far from the factory owned by Joshua Stevens. There, in 1883, he acquired a 2,000 square foot structure at 86 Broadway and commenced business with 30 employees.

Prospering, Overman expanded his factory to some 40,000 square feet and by 1891 was employing more than 1,000 workers and even had his own marching band with a full-time manager. In that year, he was so brave as to offer a prize of $10,000 to anyone who could prove that another manufacturer made more of its bicycle components in-house than he. A few years later, inspired by the developments of the Duryea brothers only a short distance away, Overman commenced making his own automobiles under the name of Victor. Wisely, he did not attempt to challenge the world on the number of components made in-house on this venture. However, the costs of personal overexpansion combined with nationwide hard times became too much for him in 1897 and before the year was out he had filed for bankruptcy. Though optimistic announcements were made early in 1898, the business was soon liquidated for the benefit of a number of creditors led by the Springfield National Bank. Overman himself left the country in 1901 and moved to London, while much of the factory structure was acquired by the Stevens firm and soon used to house the burgeoning Stevens-Duryea facility. Overman was among the first but by no means the last of the world's automobile makers to become overextended and lose his shirt.

Harry Austin Knox was born in nearby Westfield, Massachusetts, on January 19, 1875, the son of a plumber. In 1894 he graduated from Springfield's Technical Institute and the following year built his own four-cylinder gasoline engine along the Benz pattern. He followed this up with a further design of an automobile chassis to go with the engine, under contract to the Overman Bicycle Company. For Overman, Knox also built a variety of other gasoline engines, including the first American-made design to use the later universal "jump-spark" ignition system. Fortunately for Knox, he was always paid in cash and thus not caught up in the Overman bankruptcy.

In 1898, when Overman's business collapsed, the young inventor went out on his own with the Knox Automobile Company of Springfield which soon offered a line of air-cooled gasoline-powered vehicles of all descriptions. His 1901 three-wheeled runabout models offered tillersteering, a one-cylinder, air-cooled engine with a two-speed planetary transmission, and pneumatic tires. In 1902, a

III. The Duryeas, Stevens and Automobile Manufacturing

Knox car with Knox at the wheel won — hands down — the newly founded Automobile Club of America's first "reliability" contest on a run from New York to Boston and back. Knox's "porcupine" engines — so named because of the cooling pegs that protruded in all directions from the engine block — were widely advertised for their unique advantage of being "waterless."

The first of the Knox vehicles were made in a factory building of the Elektron Manufacturing Company, which happened to occupy much of the same block that then housed the Springfield Trade School. Elektron itself was later acquired by the Otis Elevator Company. The same Springfield *Republican,* now a daily paper, that had announced Thomas Blanchard's automobile in 1826, noted in its edition of February 8, 1900:

> A new automobile company has recently been formed in this city to manufacture the motor wagon invented by H.A. Knox and E.H. Cutler. This is to be known as the Knox Automobile Company, and is organized with a capital stock of $50,000, with the following officers: President, W.E. Wright, Vice-president H.A. Knox, treasurer, E.H. Cutler, secretary, Albert E. Smith. The new company will lease the present plant of the Waltham Watch Tool Company [makers of watchmaking tools] when they move into their new factory. The next three or four months will be devoted to the further perfection of the automobile and the fitting up of the plant with the necessary machinery for the manufacture of the wagon. At the end of that period it is thought the company will be ready to receive orders for their machine.
>
> The automobile which is to be made is well known in the city, as it has been in constant use about the streets during the past few months. It is a three-wheeled affair, the front wheel being used to steer with. All the machinery is placed out of sight beneath the body of the wagon, and the power is furnished by a three-horsepower gasoline engine. The automobile can be run at a high rate of speed, and has been run at 30 miles an hour. The steering lever is controlled by the right hand, while the speed is governed by the left, and the brake is worked by a foot lever. The strong feature of the vehicle is its extreme simplicity and ease of control.

Knox stayed with the air-cooled concept, one of only five car makers in America to do so, most other manufacturers having switched by 1910 to the more complicated but more effective liquid cooling for their engines. His advertising made much of the simpler design that these engines offered — particularly noting the saving on coolants and the complexities of pumps, radiators and hoses that watercooling necessarily entails. A subsidiary, the Knox Motor Truck Company, was organized in 1904 and made a series of early fire engines, starting with several for the City of Springfield. Knox also made the first trucks to be bought by the United States Army. It was an omen! In 1918, the inventor sold all his automotive interests, most products of which were now being manufactured by the Lyons Atlas Company of Indianapolis, and took a management position in the Ordnance Department of the United States Army.

In time, Harry Knox rose to become the head automotive engineer for the Department, in which capacity he developed dozens of patents on transmissions, spring suspensions, steering devices and drive systems for the American tanks made for the Allies during World War II. Knox never became involved in the disputes between other automobile makers about priority of invention, etc. His continued use of air-cooling made him directly competitive with only one other long-lived auto maker, the H.H. Franklin Automobile Manufacturing Company of Syracuse, New York.

Meanwhile, back in Springfield, cars were still being built. With the liquidation of the Knox business locally, the automotive plant on Waltham Avenue, which was only a few hundred feet from that of the famous Indian Motorcycle Company, now lacked a tenant. Into that vacuum stepped the venerable English automotive firm that had been founded in 1902 by the 32-year-old aviation pioneer Charles Stewart Rolls and the slightly older electrical designer, Sir Frederick Henry Royce. Rolls, who was the first person to fly the round trip across the English Channel, died in an airplane crash in 1910 (Great Britain's first air fatality) but Royce, now close to 60 years old, continued to take an active part in the business. However, in the harsh economic climate that afflicted England after the Great War of 1914–18, the export of royalty-paying technology was permitted, but not that of capital investment.

The English car maker had already achieved a certain upper class cachet in America as the manufacturer of the most expensive and sophisticated motor vehicle chassis in the world. Despite the fact

III. The Duryeas, Stevens and Automobile Manufacturing

that, regardless of where sold, they were all built with the increasingly atypical right-hand drive — or perhaps because of the added touch of exclusivity which such ownership provided to those able to afford them — these cars had become a symbol associated with financial success and social status around the world. They were thus a notch in prestige above the home-grown American competition no longer supplied by Stevens-Duryea but still offered by Cadillac, Chrysler, La Salle, Packard, and Pierce-Arrow. But to make them in England, ship them overseas and then pay duty on their import to America was a severe and additional economic disincentive. Because of the post-war isolationism and protectionism sentiment then rampant in America, which culminated in the Smoot-Hawley Act of 1930 which many people subsequently blamed for the onset of the Great Depression, it was decided that Rolls-Royce cars should be made in America. Production would be done, however, to the same exacting standard of workmanship that had made their name a byword for quality in Europe.

The Knox factory on Waltham Avenue and many of the skilled machinists who had been employed there were available. While the settlement terms of the recent war were still being argued over in Paris, the decision was announced on September 22, 1919, to locate a branch factory in Springfield. The British firm made it clear in their press statement that Springfield was selected primarily because "the Springfield Arsenal and other industries in the area provided a pool of manpower skilled in precision metalworking." In addition that city was found to be conveniently located between two of the largest potential market areas for sale of such moving symbols of opulence, Boston and New York. And finally, statistics from the federal government were cited which showed that the Springfield area, of all major communities, was freest from "labour difficulties."

An American subsidiary with total available capital of nearly $6 million was formed and arrangements were soon made to obtain the necessary factory space. In time, this also came to include another set of buildings a mile to the north in East Springfield, some of which had housed elements of Stevens-Duryea production in its dying years and others of which had been constructed for the final assembly and storage of World War I tanks by the United States Army. Early in 1920, the American auto-buying public was informed:

> A limited number of Rolls-Royce chassis will be produced at the American works. These will be identical and interchangeable with the chassis produced at the works in Derby, England. Production operations are under direct supervision of trained experts from the English works. No bodies will be produced. Rolls-Royce policy is to build the chassis only. The same quality of materials will be employed as in England.
>
> The production in America is being carried on as an important phase of Rolls-Royce, Ltd. It is not in any way an attempt to capitalize or trade on the Rolls-Royce prestige. F. Henry Royce is Engineer in Chief of the American operations and a member of the Board of Directors in America. Claude Goodman Johnson, a managing director of Rolls-Royce, Ltd., is Chairman of the Board in America and makes regular trips to America. The product of the American works will be drawn upon for English as well as American patrons. The interests of present Rolls-Royce owners in America will be protected and safeguarded by American production.

While patently self-serving and just a trifle misleading, this announcement heralded the future production of 2,944 motor vehicles from the two Springfield locations, one of which was soon devoted to production of car bodies, after arrangements with Brewster & Company of Long Island City, New York, were found to be inadequate. Fifty-three foremen and supervisors, complete with their families and possessions, were brought over from Derby, many of whom stayed on in other American capacities after the plant was closed shortly after the onset of the Great Depression. One of these expatriates even became the personal chauffeur to the mayor of Springfield, but then had to drive a Pierce-Arrow. Soon after beginning production in Springfield, Rolls-Royce cars began to carry American components, such as the American Bosch coils (also made in Springfield) that replaced the Watford ignitions of English make which had proven to be less reliable. American-made wheels replaced those supplied by Dunlop. The plant manager, Maurice Olley, who later went on to design suspension systems for General Motors, even went so far as to change the design of the Springfield-

III. The Duryeas, Stevens and Automobile Manufacturing

made Rolls-Royce from the genteel snobbishness of right-hand drive to the more practical — in America, anyway — left-hand drive. This did not involve a great deal of re-engineering but the process might have been advanced by the plant manager's personal experiences in getting around town, on which Olley waxed poetic:

> The streetcars of Springfield, they come and they go,
> They get there at last, tho' a trifle slow;
> When you're out in your auto and try to get past,
> That's the only occasion on which they go fast.

When this author was growing up and learning to outrace on his bicycle the streetcars of Springfield, it was common knowledge that the engines produced at the community's Rolls-Royce factory required none of the customary gaskets, unanimously used by other car makers, between the engine block and the cylinder head as well as between other components within the power train. The engines and transmissions made at the factory on Waltham Avenue were machined with such precision that gaskets would have been a hindrance to effective operation of the engine, rather than a necessity. Alas, the Great Depression put an end to such quality workmanship and — with the exception of a batch of 135 cars made in the otherwise closed factory to the personal design and order of Edsel Ford in 1934 — automobile manufacturing in the community where American automobiles were made, albeit intermittently, since 1826 was over.

The Stevens-Duryea

Percival Lowell's car was far from the first product in the Stevens-Duryea lineup; "Model Y" implied that much of the alphabet had been used beforehand. In fact, the "Y" was close to the last model designed before J. Frank Duryea had a nervous breakdown and was forced to retire from an active part in the production of automobiles. At close to the same time, the Stevens people also lost interest in the business; with a war on in Europe the gun game was better than ever. Production was erratic thereafter and then what little was left went to the heirs of George Westinghouse.

The earliest Duryea prototype automobile was produced in 1891 and had steel tires on wooden rims with a separate chain drive for each of the rear wheels. This latter concept was taken straight from the bicycle and lingered on, particularly in heavier vehicles like trucks, for several decades. However, the original American car had a total weight of only 700 pounds. It carried acetylene lamps for both front and rear, with 44-inch diameter wheels on the front and 48-inch wheels on the rear. While acetylene gives a brilliant light, the process of feeding the gas container and then individually lighting each fixture is time consuming in the extreme. The auto's one-cylinder, four-cycle engine was water-cooled and could move the vehicle along, complete with driver and passenger, at the grand sustained speed of 10 miles per hour.

IV. The Stevens-Duryea

The 1893 model that actually ran on the streets of Springfield was quite similar. Its major differences consisted in having the chain drive system include only one such rear axle sprocket and the great leap forward of being shod with Dr. Dunlop's recently developed pneumatic tires—all of three inches in tube diameter and made just down the river in Hartford. However, the running lights had disappeared.

The 1897 model, which Charles took with him back to Peoria and later to Reading, boasted three cylinders and three wheels with an engine having a 4½-inch bore and an 8-inch stroke. The body of the companion four-wheeled model was now doubly spring-mounted, but over the heavier-duty rear wheels only. However, the running lights had returned and the pneumatic tires were now of four-inch cross-section and gave a better ride, though still requiring 60 pounds per square inch. In paying for these improvements, the Duryea brothers were not much different from other automobile entrepreneurs. Their first car had been bankrolled by Edwin F. Markham of Springfield, who later became treasurer of the United States Automatic Lighting Company. The brothers' second car was financed by insurance executive Henry W. Clapp (1854–1926). And their third, the car which won the Chicago race (see below), was bankrolled by George H. Hewitt, originally a mining engineer, who stayed with the automotive idea and later became an executive with Stevens-Duryea.

Then came the breakup. With the benefit of hindsight, it is obvious from his future actions that Charles wanted the firm to take the route of smaller, lower-priced vehicles, soon to be made popular by the likes of Henry Ford and Louis Chevrolet, while Frank was more interested in an upscale market, then widely perceived to be the only prospects for these machines. Interestingly, as president of Princeton University in 1906, Woodrow Wilson gave a backhanded endorsement to this view by forbidding the presence of automobiles on his campus because of the fear that "they would excite socialist envy," among the townsfolk.

Soon after the separation of the brothers, Frank, and his chief draftsman, William Remington, moved their place of business a mile east of downtown Springfield to 837 State Street, while they worked out their deal with Stevens Arms. This firm was flush with profits from arms sales made during the recent Spanish-American War, but that war was now over and their factory no longer fully occupied with those contracts. On August 29, 1901, the business deal was made whereby Frank and his associates would design the product and receive a share of the profits while the Stevens Company would underwrite the process and do the actual fabrication of the automobiles. (This entry of an arms maker into a civilian business was much akin to the process whereby the arms making company started in Springfield in 1829 by James Tyler Ames and his younger brother, Nathan — acquired in 1845 by Eliphalet Remington — branched out into the manufacture of agricultural equipment such as shovels and in 1873 started the production of typewriters.)

After the deal with the Stevens company closed, all operations ceased in Springfield and production of the Stevens-Duryea four-passenger "Stanhope" model was commenced on October 1, 1901, in that firm's Chicopee Falls factory. This body style name derives from that of Charles Stanhope, the third Earl of Chesterfield (1753–1816), a prominent English politician who advocated Parliamentary reform, peace with the American colonies and elimination of slavery. The earl also spent much of his time in scientific research and is credited with the invention of a form of microscope, a printing press and an early steam carriage. The first Stevens-backed vehicles were very nearly the same style of machine that Charles was to continue making for the next dozen years, but Frank's larger and more opulent concepts, now possible to produce under greatly enhanced financial aegis, were to evolve substantially and become the industry pacesetters. Stevens-Duryea made almost fifty cars during 1902.

Over the next several years, the combination was so successful that Stevens Arms & Tool Company found itself reaping far more profit from automobile-making than from its traditional product lines. In 1904, the precedent-setting Model "R" was introduced which featured a vertically mounted, four-cylinder engine, with a dry-disc clutch and an integrated transmission that was bolted together as a unit. This unitized feature was to remain the standard design for the rest of the company's days, and its three-point attachment to the automobile body and wheels remains one of Big Red's most

IV. The Stevens-Duryea

Stevens-Duryea's first "light six" automobile produced only 35 horsepower — 1908.

endearing as well as noticeably comfortable running features. Though looked upon with apprehensive disapproval by other car makers of that day, the idea was popular with the public and sold so briskly that it was soon adopted by several other auto makers. At $2,500 per car, this move proved to be a very profitable venture for the company.

One year later, Stevens-Duryea again startled the automotive world by bringing out America's first six-cylinder engine advertised as the "Model S, Big Six." This substantial improvement in automotive power was first introduced to the world by the Spijker Brothers of Trompenburg, Netherlands, who had built the original six-cylinder engine for a racing car in 1903. Despite feared public apprehension at such a radical departure from the prior maximum norm of four cylinders, a slightly smaller version, the Model "U" Light Six was introduced in 1907. This was another outstanding success and corporate profits for the year exceeded a million dollars — an American automotive landmark.

The Model "X," which came out in 1909, along with the Model

Percival Lowell's Big Red Car

J. Stevens Arms & Tool Company — 1921 (photograph by R. F. Dillingham).

"Y," were revised versions of what had now become the company's standard-bearers — the Big Four and the Big Six. Dr. Lowell's big red car was a Model "Y," with a wheelbase more than twice that of the Duryea Brothers' first motor vehicle. In moving toward ever larger vehicles, Stevens-Duryea was setting a trend that was to be followed by most of the rest of the industry. Of those then in the industry who were to survive, only Henry Ford deviated seriously from this trend. He aimed to bring the automobile within the reach of every American, starting with his own employees, a goal which others believed not attainable. The validity of Ford's thinking, however, was shown by the fact that his

J. Stevens Arms & Tool Company band — 1907.

IV. The Stevens-Duryea

Clockwise from top left: Stevens-Duryea factory —1902; vehicles lined up for a test drive —1905; engines powered the entire factory during break-in —1905; Noyes W. Fisk's tire factory in Chicopee, later part of United States Rubber Company —1912.

famous Model T, introduced for sale in the fall of 1909, outsold by millions anything else on the market and went fundamentally unchanged for the next nineteen years. While Ford's famous assembly line concept was not introduced until 1913, an unwanted proof of early success in his production methods was that he had already encountered shipping space problems for his automobile exports to Europe.

Duryea's Model "Y," with its molded aluminum

Factory sketch of Model "Y."

body panels, bore a great resemblance to the earlier Model "S," but its headlamps were now placed higher and to the side of the engine's hood, rather than in front of everything as previously. Necessity in the form of a few "front enders" had obviously reared its ugly head. The tires still required a relatively high pressure, and those for the

Clockwise from top left: An early version of Stevens-Duryea "Big Six" with windshield down, 1910; the original "Light Six" had no windshield—1909; the "Big Six" Model "S" seven passenger touring car—1910; *Bottom:* Comparison of the Stevens-Duryea "four" with the two "sixes"—1910.

IV. The Stevens-Duryea

Clockwise from top left: Model "U" Light Six—1910; The "Light Six" with limousine body—1909; The Stevens-Duryea four, "the 20th century hustler"—1909; The Stevens-Duryea four, as a limousine—1909.

front wheels were an inch smaller in outside diameter than those for the rear, but their wooden-spoked wheels and rims were interchangeable. The crankcase was unitary in the sense that it was of one piece of metal, but its internal subdivision into six partially separate sumps, one for each piston's connecting rod to splash into, was necessary to keep oil for each bearing close at hand because of the relatively large length of the total powerplant. One look under the hood of a Model "Y" or any other Duryea-made car discloses the exact presence of each cylinder—rather large and low pressure chambers by modern standards and reminiscent of #10 cans, but with double ignition and very easy to locate. Driver-mechanics, such as Percival Lowell's assistant Carl Lampland was to become, needed few manuals to see everything that was worth seeing on these models.

The Model "Y," delivered in various curb weights from 2,750 up to 3,800 pounds, continued to be the "top of the line" from its introduction in 1909 until 1912, though the company brought out several other models in its final years. These included the Model "AA," a "light six" touring car in 1910 and the 1913 Model "C," with a six-cylinder engine in both a 131 and a 138-inch wheelbase in several different body styles. The company's final product was the Model "D," a touring car with a smoothly rounded rear deck into which the convertible roof could totally disappear. In this process, Stevens-Duryea continued to be the style leader of the American automotive industry, setting a trend considerably at variance with the more box-like bodies of most of the others. All these models came with a fold-down windshield, which was also capable of folding only halfway. The windshield itself was a necessary refinement that even the notoriously low-cost auto maker Henry Ford had found necessary to offer on his Model B in 1904. The widespread adoption of this feature also brought about a reduction in the routine placement of Murine ads in automotive magazines.

Satellite business firms grew up around the primary automobile maker. The German-owned Bosch Company started an American subsidiary to make magnetos only two miles away in the Brightwood district of Springfield's North End. The Moore Drop Forging Company located near the American Bosch factory initially to make automobile frame components. In 1886 Noyes W. Fisk acquired the failed tire business firm of Spaulding & Pepper in Chicopee and sold tires, first to Overman, then to Stevens-Duryea. By 1904 it was the leading tire maker of the nation and later became the major component of the United States Rubber Company.

Nineteen fourteen was to be the last full year of production for all Duryea automotive products. Charles had already stopped production of his three-cylinder machines in Pennsylvania, and when operating capital was needed for production of further models in Chicopee Falls, Frank would not agree to the lenders' demands that Stevens-Duryea produce vehicles that could enter the mass market in competition with the likes of Henry Ford and now Louis Chevrolet (backed by the managerial genius of William Durant). Duryea's pride in being the engineering and style leader, even if it were deemed

IV. The Stevens-Duryea

to be the less profitable course for the company, was a severe stumbling block to those who could see only the latest balance sheet and operating statements. Stimulated by illness, J. Frank opted to retire.

Another major factor was the war in Europe. The senior management of Stevens Arms was devoting its attention to what they knew how to do best — make small arms. A sale of the automotive business was finally arranged to the Westinghouse Company, which had used and very much expanded an additional Stevens-Duryea factory in East Springfield prior to the outbreak of war in Europe. While the great inventor George Westinghouse died in 1916, as late as 1923 there were sporadic episodes of automobile production while receivers and lawyers wrangled over the corporate cadaver that remained after its guiding genius withdrew. The receivers' final account was rendered on November 24, 1924, and all assets passed on to a variety of creditors and hopeful opportunists, none of whom ever revived the grand old name and product of America's first auto makers.

By the end of the 20th century, everything was gone. Stevens Arms had been absorbed into Savage Arms; Overman was long since effectively subsumed into Stevens-Duryea. Knox had given way to Rolls-Royce and that factory was a dying memory. Westinghouse production of refrigerators had ceased, though the buildings remained in use by other firms. In Chicopee, the United States Rubber Company tire factory had closed, and even the magneto maker, American Bosch, was gone. Across the river in West Springfield, the Gilbert & Barker Company that made gasoline station pumps was gone. Even the Springfield Armory, the start of everything and where Blanchard had worked, was now only a museum, run by the National Park Service. Every scintilla of the American automobile business in the community where it had begun had disappeared.

The Great Race

In 1895, Frank Duryea had won America's first automobile race — a distinction he cherished for the rest of his life. Inspired by the initial reports on the Paris to Bordeaux automobile race in France, earlier that summer, 42-year-old Herman Henry Kohlsaat, publisher of the Chicago *Times-Herald*, announced that he would put up $5,000 in prize money for a similiar contest and cover a lot of the ancillary costs as well. The first prize would be $2,000, with lesser amounts going to various other runners-up. The event was scheduled to take place on November 2, on the streets of Greater Chicago from Hyde Park to Evanston. However, on the announced date, of the eighty advance registrants, only two vehicles were on hand: the Duryeas' third automobile, with room for only Frank, and a larger (but still single-cylindered) Benz-made car entered by Hieronymus Mueller, a brass goods manufacturer of nearby Decatur, Illinois. The competition vehicle had hard rubber tires on wooden wheels and seats for the driver and three passengers in a style then called vis-à-vis, which placed those seated in the front of the vehicle facing to the rear.

The idea had been placed in Kohlsaat's mind by his occasional columnist and science editor, Boston-born Frederick Upham (Grizzly) Adams, who was then serving as smoke inspector in charge of cleaning up the atmosphere in the then notoriously coal-smoky city of Chicago. Adams had credibility! In 1886, at age 27, he had invented the electric lamppost, which was rapidly replacing gas-fired street

V. The Great Race

lamps in American cities. An all purpose researcher, he had just published an opus entitled *Atmospheric Resistance and Its Relation to the Speed of Railway Trains*. He then came up with the design for an experimental streamlined train for the Baltimore and Ohio Railway that was to break all existing speed records in 1900. Adams had studied accounts of the 78.5 mile, Paris to Rouen automobile race of July 22, 1894, in which 21 vehicles competed, and was very aware of Emile Levassor's startling success a year later in driving solo the entire 732 miles from Paris to Bordeaux (via Orléans, Tours and Poitiers) in 48 hours, 48 minutes. Levassor came in six hours ahead of the next entry, averaging just under 12 MPH.

Since there so little competition turned out on the day originally scheduled, Kohlsaat, rather than disappoint the numerous spectators who had lined the route, announced that he would offer a preliminary "dry run" between the two vehicles on hand. It would take the form of a round-trip race to Waukegan and back. He would reschedule the main event for three weeks later. At first things went well for the American entry. Being lighter it got off to a faster start, and its lead was enhanced when the Mueller-Benz car lost a rear tire which held it up for an additional seven minutes. Then the first disaster struck: one of the driving chains broke, and the Benz-built car passed the immobile Duryea. Making a quick repair, Frank was rapidly gaining ground when a farmer pulled his wagon across the road immediately ahead of him. Having now attained a speed of more than 15 miles an hour, the Duryea vehicle's momentum was such that its brakes could not bring it to a quick enough stop and Frank could only head for the ditch, or plow into the team and laden wagon. Unfortunately, the impact of caroming off the bottom of the ditch cracked the differential gear housing, putting the American car out of the race for good. The Benz entry imported by Mueller and driven by his son, Oscar, was a clear winner. But this was only the preliminary.

Quickly shipped back to Springfield for repair, the Duryea returned west in three weeks accompanied by Frank and some of his backers, who were equally anxious to see their vehicle prove it was as a good as anything produced in Europe. Because of its lighter weight, the four horsepower of the Duryea engine could easily bring the American entry to a speed of 20 MPH. Everyone on hand felt that the upcoming Thanksgiving Day race would be decided between the same two vehicles. Nevertheless, there was now a considerably larger field than before. However, the weather was not as promising. Several inches of wet snow had fallen during the previous night and the poorly paved and barely drained highways were covered with slush and mud, while drifts and snow banks lined much of the race course.

Of the numerous entries now on hand, the owners of only eleven declared themselves willing to risk the now hazardous route. Before the race began three more of them lost confidence and withdrew from the contest. By the time the starting gun was fired, two more entries had collapsed, unable to get up to the line. That left six. Two of them were front wheel driven electric vehicles, the "Electrobat" entered by the New York firm of Morris & Salom, and the "Sturges," a short-lived Chicago-made product. Of the four gasoline-driven vehicles, three had engines made by Benz and imported from Germany, and had been entered only for the publicity value that would be gained by their sponsors. Of these vehicles, one was the winner of the "dry run" of earlier in the month, registered again by the same Mueller importing firm of Decatur; another one-cylinder vehicle was the product of its American assembler, the De La Vergne Refrigeration Company of New York. The final competing entry was the Macy-Roger, a short-lived product offered by the Strauss brothers, soon to acquire full control of the famous New York retailing firm founded in 1858 by Rowland Hussey Macy. In order to keep all contestants honest, an outside "umpire" was assigned to ride with each vehicle and driver. Mueller drew the noted Civil War hero Charles King of Milwaukee while Frank drew the well-known Canadian newspaperman Arthur Walter White, of Toronto.

The Duryea car weighed in at a gross total of 1,208 pounds: 729 for the car, 165 for the driver, 46 for the requisite gasoline, oil and water, and the balance of 268 pounds for the not inconsiderable bulk of the umpire.

For all of his personal dimensions, umpire White described the race in concise and impartial terms:

V. The Great Race

We left the starting point at 8:55 and ran without a stop to the corner of Erie and Rush Streets. Here we broke our steering gear running over a high crossing covered with snow. A wait of fifty-five minutes ensued. From this point to Evanston, we ran without a stop, arriving there at 12:35 o'clock. On the return we were delayed four minutes in Chicago Avenue, Evanston, by a sleigh that tipped over in the street. Continuing, we got into the wrong road on account of the absence of a sign at Lawrence Avenue and Clark Street. We ran down Clark to Diversey Street before discovering our mistake. Then we went up Diversey to Lincoln Avenue, and on Lincoln Avenue to Roscoe Street where we resumed the correct route. I estimated the extra distance travelled at two miles, approximate. While on Diversey near Clark we broke our "sparker" and spent fifty-five minutes repairing it. At 3:10 we resumed the journey. We were delayed fifteen minutes at Drake Avenue and Central Park Boulevard to adjust the machinery and refuel. Numerous slight delays of a minute or so I have not mentioned.

Three and one-half gallons of gasoline, and nineteen gallons of water were consumed. No power outside the vehicle was used. I estimate that enough power was used to run the motor 120 miles over smooth roads. We finished at 7:18, and ran back to Sixteenth Street with our power.* Our correct[ed] time was seven hours and fifty-three minutes. We covered a distance of 54.36 miles—averaging a little more than seven miles per hour.

Assuming umpire White's odometer and stopwatch were accurate and read correctly, his arithmetic was slightly off the mark. The correct speed was actually 6.89556 MPH. However, when all the entries had been accounted for—some of them did not leave the starting line and three others did not finish the course—there ensued four hours of deliberation; one wonders what Windy City watering hole was the site of this time-consuming process. At the end of their intellectual peristalsis, the judges divided up the prize money among those who made it as far as the starting line, as follows: $2,000 to the Duryea Motor Wagon Company, the undeniable winner, for its overall superior performance and economy of operation; $1,500 to H. Mueller, the runner-up (who stayed in business for another five years, building his own car bodies, though powered always by Benz engines);

---

*This last leg was not part of the course, but turned out to be beyond the ability of the Mueller entry.

Percival Lowell's Big Red Car

$500 each to R.H. Macy and the Sturges Electric Company, whose entries finally finished; $200 to G.W. Lewis of Chicago; $150 to Haynes-Apperson of Kokomo; $100 to Max Hertel of Chicago and $50 to De La Vergne Refrigeration. The latter four entries never got started or collapsed by the wayside.

There was more to the contest than in Umpire White's brief report. The weather was anything but congenial, and cold had forced some of the riders to abandon the contest. Two of the electrics ran out of power early on and gave up by the time they reached Lincoln Park. The De La Vergne Benz-powered car lost out to a snowdrift in Washington Park. The Macy vehicle collided with an Adams Street horsecar but was sufficiently undamaged that it continued on to Evanston, finally collapsing at Douglas Park on the return leg. One of Mueller's passengers had become so afflicted by the cold that he had to be carried from the car to a hospital at Riverview. Both the "winners" had incurred "rules violations" along the way. Duryea had to stop at a blacksmith's shop to forge a repair to the steering gear and Mueller had collapsed, unconscious from the cold, compelling umpire King to finish the course as driver. But both infractions were ignored by the judges, whose concentration was basically on the vehicular performance, not the human.

The event was heavily covered by Kohlsaat's paper, of course, but less so elsewhere. Not even White's paper carried the story. In a further sign of the automobile's insignificance in American life, the *New York Times* completely ignored the race, despite the fact that almost half the entries were from the New York area. Nevertheless, the race brought on two unforeseen consequences: It was the making of the Duryea name both in Europe and America and thereby led to the foundation of a great company; and the publicity resultant within the budding automobile circle of the United States gave great impetus to the movement for better highways in America—comparable to those of France. Heretofore this thrust had come largely from the small and not very vocal group of bicycle devotees; now it gathered a much wider public interest.

Every automobile manufacturer extolls his product—in more modern times largely by the use of television advertisements that feature the massive horsepower, smooth ride and the wondrous

V. The Great Race

financing methods available to the purchaser. As will be seen below, the makers of Stevens-Duryea cars used a somewhat more subdued tone in their sales material, but it still made the prospect think. However, they had a good measure of independent, outside support for their propaganda. Consider the following about their Model "Y" from an article that appeared in the periodical *Machinery* in October of 1909, entitled "Design and Construction of a High-Grade Motor Car":

> The following description of a 40 HP automobile, built by the Stevens-Duryea Company, of Chicopee Falls, Mass., may, except for certain important details which will be specifically mentioned, be taken as typical of the design of high-grade cars in general. In Fig. 1 is shown a side view of the "Model Y," 40 horsepower, six-cylinder machine, with 36-inch wheels and a 142-inch wheelbase. An automobile may be divided into two parts—the body and the "chassis." The former is the product of the carriage-maker's art, the latter of the mechanic's and engineer's....
>
> The mechanism and body of the car are supported by a frame whose side members, of chrome-nickel steel, are shown.... These are supported by four cross pieces, and are supported on the front and rear axles by the spring connections shown. The cross pieces are also pressed from chrome-nickel steel, and are hydraulically riveted to the side frames. A platform spring suspension is used at the rear, hung on connecting shackles designed to overcome the side roll met when rounding curves in large and fast cars. The springs are made from steel selected after careful tests of both American and imported materials. The cost of the brand selected was far in excess of that of the nearest competitor, but it gave an endurance under repeated shock and reversal of stress not met with in any other make....

The article continued for many more pages, extolling the quality of design and work that went into the Chicopee-made automobiles, and giving relatively unbiased credence to what the company said about itself. Here follows a sample of the brochure it used when Percival Lowell — having had enough of the vagaries of horse-dependent travel and diffident companionship — set out to buy one of those modern carriages for himself.

> The observing traveler in New England is always impressed by the simple dignity and enduring quality of the Colonial houses built in the days of Paul Revere. His invariable reaction is the keen desire to obtain the same sterling workmanship in articles of everyday use. From

the born artisan only, can such workmanship be secured. The descendants of the expert Colonial workers have never left New England. They have remained here building firearms, motor cars, and other products of modern day in the expert and honest manner of their forefathers. To the newcomer they have imparted their spirit of sincere craftmanship [sic] and have made their ideals his own. Those who could not grasp the craft idea have gone elsewhere.

Here in New England, where we build the Stevens-Duryea, the ideals and traditions of other days are held sacred, as they are held in no other part of our country.

Here in New England, the joy of the worker in his work still survives and flourishes; craftsmen sons of craftsmen forefathers still put character of work above questions of hours and pay.

Only in New England has this traditional craftsmanship been the heritage of large numbers of worthy sons of worthy sires.

Nowhere else in our broad land are there bodies of such workers sufficiently large to produce such motor cars in sufficient quantities to supply a nation-wide market.

A car of such superior character cannot be produced by labor, under such industrial conditions as obtain in the newer parts of the country.

But here at Stevens-Duryea there is no dearth of craft-descendants of our Colonial master-artisans who, working within infinitesimal limits, in practice establish perfection through sheer pride and joy in expressing their super-skill.

The creators of Stevens-Duryea and the artisans who reproduce the creators' ideal have endowed their product with the finest prestige enjoyed by any American-built car.

The perpetuation of this prestige is our most sacred heritage from those who inspired the Stevens-Duryea spirit in the earliest days of the motor car industry.

All honor to American genius as it has found expression in the newer parts of the country. The great blessing of standardized quantity production has brought individual motor transportation within reach of all.

But there are, and always will be in America, many who desire the product of master-craftsmen — who value the infinitely fine and accurate work of the born artisan — who wish such workmanship to have permanent utility, and therefore value the use of materials in which it can endure.

The Stevens-Duryea appeals to those who seek to possess in all things, that which has permanence.

And so, we at Stevens-Duryea put into our product not only materials that endure and workmanship that stands the test of time, but design of such *substantial dignity* and *solid worth* as defies the decrees

V. The Great Race

of changing fashions, and commands the respect due to sterling character.

And that Stevens-Duryea Motor Cars do win and hold such respect, witness the standing and character of people who own and drive them year after year — the same car for a hundred thousand miles and more — and grieve at the thought of ever giving them up, for fear that their like cannot have been reproduced.

Conditions were not ideal for racing on the day of the Duryea victory.

Such regard is of greater worth than all the material assets an industry can ever acquire. Physical property and all manner of equipment can be replaced, but such regard is of slow growth, born of rich experience, matured by years that repeat for many the same invariable experience.

It may therefore be assumed without risk, that upon each Stevens-Duryea has been expended the same infinite care and vigilance that has always endeared the Stevens-Duryea to experienced owners.

Except for the faddist, the lover of ostentatious show, or those who put striking style above obvious sterling worth, the Stevens-Duryea for all its extremes of adherence to unalterable standards, is sound, sane value for those who count final costs.

It commands the respect as no other car does, of the substantial man of ripe experience and judgement of things befitting those who themselves stand for the best and who themselves command the honor and respect of their communities.

Among this substantial element of our citizenship will always be found the owners of Stevens-Duryea Motor Cars.

Those are the chosen thousands for whom the Stevens-Duryea engineers expend their experienced ingenuity, for whom the Stevens-Duryea artisans lavish their heritage of skill, their rich training, their love of truth and beauty.

Here in New England, where the Stevens-Duryea is built, as nowhere else in the country, it is possible to produce such extravagant quality with practical economy.

Percival Lowell's Big Red Car

The product of such traditional, long perpetuated master craftsmanship can but be what it is and always has been — the most perfect, enduring example of unswerving devotion to a heritage that has found expression in the modern motor car.

STEVENS-DURYEA DEVELOPMENT

1891 • Inception of the American automobile — the foundation of the Stevens-Duryea motor car.

1892 • One-cylinder, friction transmission, chain drive. The prototype of a "horseless" era.

1894 • Two-cylinder, individual speed transmission, single-chain drive. Progress in its first stages and a long step toward the realization of the perfect motor car of today.

1895 • Winner of the Chicago Times-Herald race.

1896 • Winner of the Cosmopolitan Race, New York, and the Liberty Run, London to Brighton.

1898 • Advent of the lightweight car. Adoption of three forward speeds.

1901 • Stevens-Duryea, two-cylinder, single-chain drive cars, with three forward speeds, first placed on the market.

1904 • Four cylinder shaft drive. Adoption of "Unit Power Plant" supported on "Three Points" and embodying the dry-plate clutch (multiple disc), marking the greatest advance of motor car construction. Instantaneous success — a remarkable demonstration of Stevens-Duryea initiative and knowledge of correct mechanical principles.

1905 • Advent of the Stevens-Duryea six-cylinder car. The first to be marketed in this country and since that time the standard for high-powered motor cars.

1910 • Value and importance of Stevens-Duryea design features — The "Unit Power Plant" supported on Three Points — proven by their retention without change in six years manufacturing, and by their recent adoption by other makers.

THE BRAVE NEW WORLD OF AUTOMOBILES

Soon after the brothers made the first horseless carriage in America, a number of other people started to follow their example. Between them all they brought a great variety of innovations and improvements. But the fundamental principles of every automobile made for the next hundred years were on hand when Percival Lowell's car was designed. Some of the famous persons that Frank Duryea associated, and competed, with remain household names in North America — most of them do not.

Automobile makers were adventurers into a field that some persons thought to be fly-by-night, while others felt these pioneers might upset convention and the status quo. As either of such they did not merit serious inclusion among the business, political, professional or intellectual elite of the nation — very few of the pioneers in what became America's largest industry ever made it into *Who's Who*, dead or alive. The brothers Duryea did not! Not one of the five Mack brothers of New York (John, Augustus, William, Charles and Joseph) achieved such notice; nor did Jonathan Dixon Maxwell (1864–1928), Louis Gorham Hupp (1872–1961) and his younger brother Robert Craig, David Dunbar Buick (1854–1929), Louis Chevrolet (1878–1941), John Dodge (1864–1920) or his younger brother Horace,

Percival Lowell's Big Red Car

George Norman Pierce (d. 1910), whose Buffalo-made cars won the second, third, fifth and sixth American automobile endurance races, or a host of other equally deserving persons, some of whom are mentioned below.

On the other hand, Howard Carpenter Marmon (1876–1943), who won the first Indianapolis 500 race, on May 30, 1911, at an average speed of 74.61 MPH did rate such elite inclusion. However, he is accompanied by a number of other individuals such as the Ottawa Indian chief Pontiac (1720–1769), Hernando De Soto (1500–1542), Fr. Robert Cavelier, Sieur de La Salle (1643–1687), Antoine de la Mothe, Sieur de Cadillac (1660–1730), and even George Washington (1732–1799) and Abraham Lincoln (1809–1865), all of whom had nothing to do with the American automobile industry, but have still received very substantial recognition in it.

Ohio-born Ransom Eli Olds was 46 years of age when Percival Lowell's car was made. He had begun his business career as a bookkeeper in his father's Lansing machine shop in 1883 and joined him as a partner two years later. He followed some of the same concepts as Thomas Blanchard in evolving a steam-powered, self-propelled vehicle. But Olds, who had made a number of stationary engines, used gasoline only in the burner to heat the water for his boiler. In the United States in those days this fluid was a by-product of distillation from crude oil of the less volatile kerosene that was in great demand for home heating, cooking, and various applications of artificial lighting. Gasoline was unwanted, therefore cheap; but it was occasionally quite difficult to handle and in certain situations its volatile and explosive nature presented safety problems. By contrast, gasoline in Europe, where as yet little petroleum had been located, was considerably scarcer — a condition which led a number of the earlier European manufacturers to the use of alternative fuels.

Olds' first successful elimination of the horse came in 1887, but he, like Blanchard 60 years earlier, soon found small engine steam propulsion difficult to work with. The internal combustion engine had been evolved by several European technicians over the prior decade and had proved equal, if not superior to, steam when applied to carriages in both France and Germany. In 1896, three years after the Duryea brothers had driven their first automotive device around

VI. The Brave New World of Automobiles

the streets of Springfield, Olds loosed his first gasoline-powered horseless carriage onto the streets of Lansing, Michigan. A year later, he organized the Olds Motor Vehicle Company, which evolved in 1899 into the Olds Motor Works and was relocated to Detroit, where he made the first production model of Oldsmobile. This was the Model "R," a wooden-wheeled, solid-tired vehicle that was tiller-steered and could hold four persons. When a fire destroyed his factory, only one of the models under construction was pulled free and saved. This was a smaller vehicle with wire wheels weighing only 700 pounds and selling for $650, but it became a part of American folklore for having inspired the still popular ditty about a "merry Oldsmobile." Even Sir Thomas Lipton, the British tea magnate, acquired one. In 1904 Olds sold the business—and his name—to an emerging combination that was soon to become known as General Motors.

But Olds had not sold what he carried in his head. The very next year Americans heard about the Reo Motor Car Company, a firm whose name used his initials—which he had not sold to William Durant's company. Ransom Olds made quality cars for another ten years before relinquishing control of his second automobile company and devoting his ample energies to other activities. His greatest contribution to the industry was probably the evolution, toward the close of his automotive career, of the synchromesh transmission which largely eliminated need for the dicey practice of double clutching when shifting gears. In his later years, Olds founded the Ideal Lawnmower Company and the Capital National Bank of Detroit, and undertook an extensive real estate development near Tampa, Florida. Olds' most famous model was not the musical "Speedwagon," but the more prosaic "Flying Cloud"; his "farewell" model was his twenty-fourth, brought out in December of 1911.

Charles Franklin Kettering was born in 1876 on a farm near the small town of Loudonville, Ohio, an overgrown crossroads southeast of Mansfield. He studied engineering at Ohio State University and found his first steady job with the National Cash Register Company in Dayton. For this employer he devised the world's first electric cash register. Leaving NCR in 1909, Kettering became one of the founders of the Dayton Engineering Laboratories Company, better known in the world today by its initials. In due course Kettering's own name was applied to the Dayton suburb where Delco's original factory is situated.

This developmental firm went on in later years to evolve such products as Freon for refrigeration units and fast-drying paints for automobile finishes. It would discover the properties of tetraethyl lead to improve engine performance and eliminate the "knock" that indicated inefficient combustion. Most of these enhancements to automotive usage came after 1918 when Kettering's company was absorbed into General Motors. Despite the large number of automotive developments associated with Kettering's name, his single greatest claim to subsequent automotive fame was the evolution of the electric starter. A legendarily large number of broken arms and other injuries had resulted from the "kick" of an engine when ignition occurred in the cylinders before the hand crank could be fully disengaged. Beyond that inconvenience, prior to 1911, starting a cold engine was often an exercise that required a lot of arm-power — more than many people possessed. The evolution of more sophisticated engines with higher compression ratios only exacerbated these drawbacks. Lowell's original owners and drivers used hand-power to get Big Red's engine going until a Wagner starting motor was affixed in 1914, to be replaced more effectively late in 1998 when one of Kettering's devices was smoothly affixed onto her flywheel. This convenience had finally been offered by the Stevens-Duryea Company on their 1915 models, of which very few were ever produced, and the factory offered a retrofit for earlier vehicles.

As vice president of General Motors and chief of its research for a generation after 1920, Kettering played a major part in the evolution of high-compression gasoline engines for automobiles, and major improvements to Rudolph Diesel's type of engine that ultimately spelled the end of steam-power on the world's railroads. He then made the "stick shift" an option, rather than a necessity, with the development of the variable-speed automatic transmission that first appeared in GM's Oldsmobile line in 1937. Besides bringing these innovations and conveniences to the public, Kettering endowed Antioch College, a few dozen miles from his home in Dayton, with a foundation to study photosynthesis and chlorophyll. His name, however, probably remains best known to subsequent Americans for his larger philanthropy known as the Sloan-Kettering Institute for Cancer Research in New York City, which he founded in 1936 in cooperation with his associate in the management of General Motors, Alfred Pritchard Sloan, Jr.

The twin boys born to Solomon and Apphia (French) Stanley of Kingfield, Maine, on June 1, 1849, were named Francis Edgar and Freelan Oscar. After graduation from Bowdoin College the brothers opened a photographic studio during the operation of which they began to study the chemistry of silver nitrate, a product whose exposure to light forms the basis of all photography. In 1883, the brothers revolutionized camera operation with the evolution of the "dry" plate. This invention was later sold to George Eastman's company in Rochester, New York, who applied the concept to cellulose film.

While enjoying the fruits of their first invention the brothers became interested in the idea of automobiles, and in 1897, deep in the backwaters of Maine, used the "flash" technique evolved in 1881 by 23-year-old Leon Serpollet to produce a successful steam engine for application to a horseless carriage. The following year, they sold their first production models. Soon their business was acquired by what became the Locomobile Company. In 1902 the brothers moved to Newton, Massachusetts, reacquired their steam patents from Locomobile, and organized the more famous Stanley Motor Carriage Company. When Francis died — in an automobile accident in 1918 — Freelan was saddened and remained associated with the automobile business only briefly.

The famous Stanley Steamer burned the less volatile kerosene as a fuel and became world renowned for its speed and endurance. The small steam engine had one notable advantage over the gasoline engine in that it required minimal gear shifting and could go at increasingly faster speeds without much of this bothersome and momentum-wasting process. In 1906 Freelan had driven one of their vehicles over a one-mile course at Ormond Beach, Florida, in 28.2 seconds — the still astounding speed for normal automobiles of 125 miles per hour. In addition, Stanley cars were perennial finishers and frequent winners of the grueling 8-mile, 4,500-foot climb race up the Carriage Road to the cold and windswept summit of New

Hampshire's Mount Washington. However, neither of these brothers made it into *Who's Who* until 1923, after the death of the one and when the survivor had left the automobile business to open a hotel in Estes Park, Colorado, where he died on October 2, 1940.

James Ward Packard (1863–1928) of Warren, Ohio, had previously worked out a number of innovations in the fabrication of incandescent lamps for the Westinghouse Company and then gone out on his own in that business. In 1898 he found himself disappointed with the Winton he had just purchased and felt that with a little effort he could do a great deal better on his own. He produced his first experimental car a year later — a two-seater with 69-inch wheelbase, 34-inch wire wheels, a one-cylinder engine, and tiller steering. Packard began the serious manufacture of automobiles in 1900.

As his New York & Ohio Company grew, however, Packard remained at heart a tinkerer and spent most of his time devising improvements to carbureting, ignition and braking systems. Packard's Model "L" of 1904 showed the modern trend of a steering wheel, rather than the heretofore widespread tiller for steering. It had wooden spoked wheels and five-inch tires with a pair of flaring front mudguards. It also had the adjustable side vents on the engine's hood that became the company's trademark style feature for the next fifty years. Despite his inattention to the business side of the business, or perhaps because of the boss's obsession with enhancements, Packard cars became a nationwide symbol of quality in automobile construction, and the "H" shift that Packard designed soon became an international standard.

In 1913, Packard sold most of his equity in the company to the Detroit financier Henry Bourne Joy (1864–1936), who had bought a part interest a decade earlier; thereafter Packard stayed on only in a titular capacity. The company remained independent and profitable through the great consolidations of the 1920s that resulted in the "Big Three" and a few less important independents. Even after the merger of this company with that of the Studebaker brothers, soon after the end of World War II, Packard's cars were sold with the catchy and well-remembered slogan "Ask the Man Who Owns One." Until the final car came off the line in 1958, Packards were invariably associated with America's patrician "Four Hundred," rather than with the

VI. The Brave New World of Automobiles

plebeians that were catered to under the names of such latter day mass production auto makers as the cantankerous Henry Ford and the Swiss-born Louis Chevrolet.

Packard cars might well have survived longer in the post World War II environment but for three events: (1) the dies and molds for the company's first postwar models were given to the Soviet Union in a misplaced gesture of national generosity, an act which resulted in the Communist nation's few hundred luxury ZIS-110 series; (2) the merger with Studebaker was disastrous for Packard production; and (3) the company's prime dealership, that which had been established by former Massachusetts governor Alvin Tufts Fuller in Boston, defected to Cadillac.

Clement Studebaker was a wagon maker, born in the no longer operative hamlet of Pinetown, Pennsylvania, in 1831. Of all those who played a part in the evolution of American automobile manufacturing, he was the only one who did not live to see any real fruit from his efforts. With his older brother, Henry, in 1852 he organized the Studebaker Brothers Manufacturing Company in South Bend, Indiana. Soon joined by three other siblings, but with Clement remaining as president, this firm became the world's largest maker of wagons and carriages, finally outstripping even the historic Concord Stage Coach Company. Not until 1897, however, long after many others had gotten on the bandwagon, did the company start experimenting with other than horsepower. Their first production model automobile rolled onto the streets of South Bend after Clement's death.

The Studebaker Brothers continued in South Bend as an independent maker of a line of mid-priced cars until well after the end of World War II and were fondly remembered by a small number of GIs for their part in the war effort. Under contract to the War Department, Studebaker produced several models of tracked over-snow vehicles for use in mountain and winter warfare. In this, they were the predecessors of Quebec's Bombardier Company and a variety of smaller snowmobiles. In even later years the South Bend factory made the U.S. Army's HUMV.

In 1875, Walter Percy Chrysler was born on a farm outside of Wamego, Kansas, a crossroads town east of Manhattan on the Kansas

Percival Lowell's Big Red Car

River. His first employment was as an apprentice railroad mechanic, from which he worked his way up to become manager of the American Locomotive Company in 1912. But he saw the handwriting on the wall of railroad engineering, and that same year he left to assume a managerial position with the company that had been formed in 1902 by the Scottish-born David Dunbar Buick. Buick had started in business as a maker of plumbing parts, making his name in enameled bathtubs, and branched out from there. His automotive firm, with its distinctive valve-in-head engine, had become a segment of General Motors Corporation. In 1912 Chrysler staged a novel and interesting advertising display. He arranged for a special 50-car railroad train to take 220 Buicks from Detroit across the country to Howard Motors in San Francisco. By continued use of such smart salesmanship and insisting on impeccably good engineering in his division, in 1916 the enterprising manager earned the unprecedented salary of $500,000 as president of the Buick Division.

Chrysler left General Motors in 1920 and acquired control of the Maxwell Motor Company, founded in 1904 by Jonathan Maxwell and Benjamin Briscoe. In 1923 he added the Chalmers Motor Car Company, founded in 1910 by William James Chalmers and in 1925 the conglomeration was organized as the Chrysler Corporation. In 1928 he added the 14-year-old Dodge Brothers firm to make his company the third largest automobile maker in the nation, producing vehicles under the marques of Plymouth,* Dodge, DeSoto and Chrysler. Famous for the high quality of its engineering, the firm made Sherman and other tanks for World War II, but eventually had to be rescued from financial distress, in a government-backed bailout, forty years after its founder's death in 1940.

Walter Chrysler may be equally well known for the landmark office tower in Manhattan which he commissioned and had built during the years 1926–30. At 1,048 feet, until the Empire State Building opened the following year, it was the tallest man-made structure in the world. This office tower, constructed by the Fred T. Ley Company of Springfield and later acquired by the Springfield-based Massachusetts

---

*This name had been used twenty years earlier by an Ohio firm, but these cars were made in the former Maxwell factory.

VI. The Brave New World of Automobiles

Mutual Life Insurance Company, is adorned throughout and above by a number of stainless steel icons depicting the automotive accessories and components that had made its creator world-famous.

The Dodge brothers, Horace Elgin (1868–1920) and his four-year-older brother, John Francis, were originally bicycle makers, like so many other pioneers in the automobile business. But in 1901 they opened a machine shop in Detroit, making stove segments and later items for the burgeoning automobile business. By 1910, the Dodge Brothers were running a large auto parts business in the Hamtramck section of Detroit and supplying engines for both Henry Ford's company and Durant's Oldsmobile Division. The first car bearing their own name appeared in 1914, though they remained minority (10 percent) shareholders in Ford's motor company. That initial Dodge car had America's first all-steel body.

In 1920, both the brothers died. One of their last acts had been to bring a lawsuit against Henry Ford, charging that he had expanded his business recklessly and cut prices to the point that there was insufficient money to pay appropriate dividends to his shareholders. Despite Ford's pleadings about the public interest in lower priced cars, the court ruled that the business of a business was to return a profit to its shareholders. When Ford lost again on appeal, he announced that he was going to leave the Ford Motor Company and start a new automotive business. While personally irascible and often crude, given Ford's enormous popularity with both workers and the public, this was a horrible prospect for the other shareholders, so all seven of his minority investors capitulated and sold out to Ford—though at a handsome profit to themselves, the Dodge heirs receiving more than $25 million. In addition, the Dodges' own firm, based on the routine quality of their engines, continued to prosper.

Born in Boston in 1861, William Crapo Durant became the most important single factor in the automobile business around the world. After achieving financial success in the carriage and wagon-making business in 1904, he bought control of David Buick's company and built on it to evolve the largest automotive firm in the world. Convinced that "bigger" was probably "better," in 1908 he chartered the General Motors Corporation and merged his Buick into companies bearing such historic and ongoing automotive names as Cadillac, Oakland (which became Pontiac) and Oldsmobile.

Because he had accomplished much of this consolidation on borrowed funds, and due to the fiscal strain of his additional efforts to obtain control of a number of automotive suppliers—axles, engines, springs, lamps, paint, bodies, etc.—his lenders became nervous and forced him out of the management only two years later. Unfazed by this setback, he immediately coopted the good name of a noted automobile racer, Louis Chevrolet, and started the Chevrolet Motor Car Company. Born at La Chaux de Fonds, in northwestern Switzerland, Chevrolet (1878–1941) had first become noteworthy in 1905 when he beat the celebrated Barney Oldfield by going 68 miles per hour, six MPH faster than the last performance of the previous legend. Under Durant's leadership the new company's prompt success caused General Motors' bankers to reconsider, and the controversial and flamboyant executive was soon back in charge of the company, resuming its presidency in 1916.

Two years later Kettering's Delco and Durant's own Chevrolet were brought into the company, already the world's largest, and in 1919 Durant's firm acquired the Fisher Body and Frigidair Companies. Again GM became somewhat overextended and Durant invested heavily in his own stock—bought on margin—in an attempt to maintain the price of General Motors shares during the economic slump following the first World War. When the other large shareholders again panicked and forced him out of office in 1921, he formed his own personal Durant Motors Company. His last hurrah, however, though starting out with a production of 55,000 vehicles in 1922, was never a success, folding its doors in 1933 and causing Durant himself to file for personal bankruptcy in 1935. The founder of the world's largest automobile company was the only major player in the entire business to leave it in such personal disarray.

One of Durant's protégés was Charles Williams Nash, a farmer's boy from De Kalb County, Illinois, who rose from a day laborer to become general manager of the Durant-Dort Carriage Company of Flint, Michigan. In 1910, the 46-year-old executive was asked to assume charge of the momentarily ailing Buick Company, which he rapidly returned to profitability and then turned over to Walter

VI. The Brave New World of Automobiles

Chrysler. As president of General Motors following in the footsteps of Durant, he brought his cautious and conservative nature to a company that had become overextended under the previous expansive and unrestrained regime.

When the shareholders' and lenders' collective mood swung back, Nash left the company in 1916 and founded his own Nash Motors Company, which became one of the nation's few consistently profitable independent car manufacturers. As its chief executive officer he arranged a merger with the Kelvinator Company in 1937 and diverted his firm from automobile making to the home appliance field. His shareholders remained content with this major change in corporate direction, but the name of Nash, as the maker of a good quality, medium-priced, family car disappeared from the highways of America.

Harry Clayton Stutz (1876–1930) moved to Dayton in 1894 and, like Kettering, started to work for NCR. However, he achieved fame some years later for his 1911 Bearcat — America's home-grown sports car. These vehicles became favored by the dashing young man-about-town who was willing to take his chances with the emerging nemesis of the now motorcycle-powered policemen, to many of whom all such vehicles—unless parked — were invariably deemed to be speeding. At age 30, this native of Ansonia, Ohio, was hired by the Marion Motor Car Company to design a low-slung pleasure car. The cars he produced for this firm, later for the Ideal Motor Car Company and finally under his own name, consistently violated all the "laws" of apparent motion.

Stutz's models were mostly two-passenger convertibles (some with a rumble seat, so named because it was outside the body of the car and over the rear wheels), brilliantly colored and definitely low-slung. In the 1920s, however, Stutz left the glamorous field of sports vehicles for the more pedestrian but profitable field of taxicabs and later, airplane engines.

In 1894 John Michael Mack was hired by the carriage-making firm of Fallesen & Berry, in Brooklyn, New York. Three years later, with help from his brother, Augustus Frederick (1878–1940), he purchased the business. A year later, their next brother, William, who had been in the carriage business in Scranton, joined the firm. By

1900, the three brothers' experiments with various methods of horseless motive power had led them to concentrate their thinking on larger, heavier-duty vehicles. Their first such product was actually a bus with 40 horsepower and seats for 20 passengers. After incorporating the Mack Brothers Company in New York in 1903, the brothers made numerous models of buses under the trade name of "Manhattan."

Success, however, meant expansion and there was not enough factory space available in Brooklyn, so, in 1905, they incorporated the Mack Brothers Motor Car Company in Allentown, Pennsylvania, and took in their youngest two brothers, Charles and Joseph, as stockholders. In the early years of the 20th century, the five introduced features such as putting the driver's cab over the engine and incorporating gear shifting systems that allowed inexperienced drivers greater flexibility in shifting heavy-duty transmissions between higher and lower gear ratios without running the risk of stripping teeth off the cogs.

By 1920, nine years after Augustus had retired and moved to San Diego with Joseph, where they entered the real estate business, the name Mack was synonymous with heavy-duty trucks. Their chain-driven, hard rubber tired vehicles had become such a fixture of the American landscape and folklore that the name Mack has entered the English language as a symbol of vehicular power and ruggedness.

The automobile industry, as it took shape, owed its existence not only to its obvious pioneers, some of whom are mentioned above, but to some other persons who really had little interest in horseless carriages. That native of Dreghorn in Ayrshire, Dr. John Boyd Dunlop (1840–1921), for instance, was not the pioneer of the rubber tire. He merely saw the beauty in inducing such devices to hold captive air which would provide a further cushion against road noise and shock.

The use of rubber as a practical device for flexible footwear, waterproofing fabrics and finally carriage tires is more properly credited to Charles Goodyear (1800–1860) of New Haven, Connecticut. In 1837, after a series of experiments, he evolved the process of vulcanization (initially a process mostly of combining with sulfur),

VI. The Brave New World of Automobiles

which changed "India" rubber from a sticky substance (derived from the sap of various tropical trees and plants) that tended to dissolve in heat, into a much more durable product. His reward for this discovery was United States Patent #3,633 in 1844. Goodyear was able to obtain international patent protection almost everywhere except under the British Crown, but he nevertheless died deeply in debt. On the other hand, Benjamin Franklin Goodrich (1841–1888), another medical doctor, was able to obtain stronger financial backing and made use of Goodyear's patents to establish his name as the first American maker of rubber carriage tires in 1870.

The automobile soon brought on an almost explosive demand for rubber in Europe and North America. Meeting that demand had its costs elsewhere in the world. It has been reliably estimated that more than 10 million persons in the Congo and other colonial regions were cruelly abused and died between 1890 and 1910 in the course of supplying the white-skinned folk of the "advanced" nations with the sap of the wild rubber vine. With the Japanese occupation of Malaysia in early 1942, it was the shortage of rubber in World War II, not that of petroleum, that forced the adoption of gasoline rationing in the United States.

In addition to their cushioning effect, pneumatic rubber tires were rapidly found to increase traction on dry roadways so that automobiles could more readily be put into motion. Then came the matter of bringing them to a stop. The concept of "shoes" that could be clamped, with varying degrees of pressure from a system of levers, to a revolving wheel had reached a high degree of sophistication on horse-drawn vehicles and was well-established from the earliest days of automobiles. Then, in 1903, Malcolm Lockhead (1887–1958), born of Scots ancestry in the town of Niles, California (on the East Bay 20 miles north of San Jose), found his first employment with the short-lived White Steam Car Company of San Francisco. While there, at the age of only 17, he began to study the possibility of using flexible tubing and hydraulic fluid to activate the braking mechanisms of automobiles. By the time he finally had it right and was granted a patent in 1917, he and his two-years-younger brother, Allan Haines, had migrated south to the Los Angeles area, become aircraft makers and changed the spelling of their family name to Lockheed.

The Motoring Lowells

Wherein we meet some of Percival Lowell's relatives and determine why a fifty-five-year-old philanthropic capitalist may have decided to obtain a horseless carriage and then why he may have selected the choice he did.

The children of Augustus and Katharine (Lawrence) Lowell, Percival and his four younger siblings, reached maturity when the horseless carriage was just attracting public attention, its future status still unclear. Their generation grew up knowing how to manage horses and with an innate distrust of any device that tended to frighten that reliable means of transportation. A generation later the children of Percival's sisters grew up with an entirely different attitude toward the internal combustion engine, much in the manner of the computer age children of a century later vis-à-vis their respective parents. Percival's nephew who succeeded to the guidance of his observatory in 1927 could strip the automotive engine of his youth to its basic components and rebuild it with no manual or guidance. However, there were often unforeseen problems; while engaged in this practice with a motorboat of which he was a part owner, he managed to blow up the craft, almost drown, and burn all the hair off his head in the process. The generation after that grew up with a faster and airborne set of experiences on which to hone their eye-to-hand coordination.

VII. *The Motoring Lowells*

Members of the extended Lowell family often appear proud of their ancestral status as one of the "First Families" of New England, if not the entire nation. But along with any such perceived social éclat comes a corresponding set of restrictions on expected behavior as well as an ingrained obligation to live up to the accomplishments of their progenitors, however irrelevant or illusory such accomplishments may ultimately turn out to be. The one side of the coin has its obvious rewards; the other is sometimes more difficult to handle.

Take Percival's youngest sister, Amy, for example. She was a vigorous pioneer in women's liberation and has a global reputation as a passable author and poet — though most people who knew them both thought that her married middle sister, Elizabeth, wrote better verse. Amy was also an only occasional master of the evolving horseless carriage. One day, while driving her wondrous newfangled vehicle out from the civilized terrain of Boston into the hinterlands of the bucolic and far western township of Concord, her horseless carriage developed palpitations of some unknown nature. She was now a full 20 miles from the "Hub of the Universe" by roads that were not much improved from 140 years earlier when used by King George's redcoats marching out to expropriate the gunpowder supply of the restless colonials. Amy managed to coax her stuttering vehicle to the nearest garage, where the mechanic was soon able to diagnose its malady and even effect a repair. But he, too, was a Yankee and wanted to be sure of receiving payment for his services. After all, few women drove cars at all, and this was a large, strange-looking one whom he had never seen or heard of before. He asked Miss Lowell (1874–1925) if she had the necessary $25.75 to pay for the repair.

It turned out that she did not, and family legend records the subsequent conversation.

"But, my good fellow, I see you have one of those telephones here. Please place a call to Harvard University, in Cambridge, and ask for the President. He's my brother and he will assure you that my credit is good."

The mechanic pondered on this possibility for a minute.

"OK, lady, I'll take a chance on it. But a call to Cambridge is long distance, and you'll have to pay for that, too." So saying he turned the crank to reach the local operator and soon worked his way through the connections to the office of President A. Lawrence Lowell.

"Dr. Lowell, there's some woman out here in Concord whose car has broken down. She can't pay for it to be fixed but says that you're her brother and that you'll guarantee her credit."

"You say she claims to be my sister — I've got three of them and two are married with family chauffeurs. Where is this woman now? Can I talk to her?"

"She's across the road, sir, sitting on the stone wall and smoking a cigar. I'll go get her."

"Oh! In that case don't bother; that's my sister, all right. She's good for it."

Lawrence (1856–1943), the Harvard president from 1909 to 1933 and an authority on constitutional government, particularly that of Great Britain, was as distinguished as Percival. He had been named for his maternal grandfather, Abbott Lawrence, who had been a welcomed ambassador to England in the mid-19th century, but had died a few months before his namesake grandson was born. A one-year-younger brother of Percival, he too finally acquired a horseless carriage, and — being at least as masculine as Amy — liked to prove that he was as good at controlling the machine as his hired man. Unfortunately, he was not. One summer day he set out to drive to Boston from Cotuit, on Cape Cod, where he had acquired an immense tract of land he called Knomet (now the Lawrence Lowell State Forest), and a summer home overlooking the waters of Nantucket Sound. His legal domicile was on Marlborough Street in the Back Bay of Boston, but en route thereto, he proceeded straight through one of those evolving traffic-control devices called a "red light" in the town of Attleboro. Vast confusion ensued and an observant nearby policeman blew his whistle thereby causing Dr. Lowell to lurch his car to a stop.

"You've caused a serious accident, sir," the policeman said according to often told family legend. "Let me see your driver's license and vehicle registration." (Massachusetts, the cradle of American freedoms, was far ahead of the rest of the nation in requiring its citizens to adhere to such bothersome and liberty-limiting formalities.)

The officer studied the documents but was singularly unimpressed by the prominence of his apprehendee and wrote up his ticket

VII. The Motoring Lowells

fulsomely. Then he turned to the offending but by now thoroughly chagrined dignitary and told him there would doubtless be a fine if not a court appearance, perhaps even a license suspension. Returning eventually, and decidedly more carefully, to his home, Dr. Lowell, a lawyer by training and thus an officer of the court, promptly paid the stipulated fine and was told by his friends that he should consider himself lucky to have gotten off so easily.

However, only a few months later, he repeated the offense with equally catastrophic results, at a different but nearby intersection. In those days when radio equipment was cumbersome and correspondingly rare, blue police call boxes were prominent on many street corners. This time, the arresting officer took Lowell's driver's license and registration over to the nearest such box and called in the name and address of his capture. He soon found out about the prior offense and returned to the parked car.

"Mr. Lowell, you've got a record in the Plymouth County Court and were fined six weeks ago for almost the same offense."

"Yes, officer, I know."

"Well, this time, sir, I'm sure you'll lose your driving license. We can't have dangerous people on the highways, you know."

'Please, officer; you know I am the president of Harvard University."

"Yes, sir, I've heard of you. But, your driving record is what counts here." (It was an unusual person in those years who had not heard of A. Lawrence Lowell, chairman of a special 1927 "blue ribbon" panel appointed by Massachusetts Governor Fuller to review the facts and fairness of the world-famous murder and robbery trial of the self-confessed anarchists Nicola Sacco and Bartolomeo Vanzetti.)

"Officer, it would never do for it to be known that the president of Harvard had his driving license revoked. Could I make an arrangement with you?"

"If it's a bribe, sir, that's a criminal offense."

"Not a bit. If I promise you never to drive a car again, do you suppose you could overlook this offense?"

The officer, clearly a man of some perception, sized up his capture as a man of integrity and saw merit in trusting him to implement his side of such a bargain. President Lowell found his way to a telephone and called for his professional chauffeur to bring a friend and come fetch him. His driving license was never revoked, but he never drove a car on the public ways of Massachusetts again.

Three generations after his death, the folklore of Northern Arizona is replete with legends about Percival Lowell — and, like most legends, portions of them are true. The patrician, erudite, world traveler who settled atop pine-covered Mars Hill was a far cry from the rough and tumble ranchers and loggers that dominated the local gentry of northern Arizona. He did not quite belong, yet he was an acknowledged and respected celebrity and, after his death, has been

Percival Lowell (left) and Professor Edward Sylvester Morse on the Bright Angel Trail in the Grand Canyon — 1908 (Lowell Archives).

VII. The Motoring Lowells

generally acclaimed as the man who put the city of Flagstaff on the world map. During his life, however, one rancher, a member of the Flagstaff City Council, even tried to get the community to rescind its five-acre grant of land for his observatory because Lowell had erected fences to keep stray cattle out of his vegetable garden.

Such political harassment notwithstanding, the *Coconino Sun* of September 22, 1911, under the banner headline of "Political Pot Now Commences to Simmer," discussed a variety of candidacies, indicating its very Republican leanings, then noted that:

> In spite of the many general declarations for the United States senatorship from Arizona, there has been an under-current of opinion that one man especially equipped with mental ability recognized world-wide would be a most suitable first representative in the senate from Arizona — a man who has in reality made the name of Arizona known to the whole scientific world — Dr. Percival Lowell. Dr. Lowell has made no overtures to the political world, but there are persistent rumors that if Arizona honored Dr. Lowell, Dr. Lowell would be an honor to the new-born state and bring it into its own by the direct route of having the senate with him to commence with. Dr. Lowell is not an avowed candidate and is exceedingly chary of mentioning the subject.

Several pre-automobile legends have Lowell arriving in town at midnight, stepping off the train and then carrying his baggage across Front Street to the lobby of the Bank Hotel* where he would sit in sporadic conversation with the night manager until sufficient daylight that he could order a carriage to come down from Mars

The Bank Hotel, Flagstaff's finest — 1895 (Lowell Archives).

*"The Leading Hotel of Northern Arizona, T.J. Coalter, Prop." is still extant as a structure, but no longer a hotel. It now contains a variety of retail businesses with offices on the second floor.

Hill and take him up to his home. Another version of this story is a bit vague as to exactly when, but deals with Lowell's inability to telephone the observatory for a ride until the town's switchboard operators reported for work at 8 A.M. Other legends, of a later date, have him walking down from his "low mesa" to go about his errands in town until met by his driver, Gormley, and then being driven back up the hill in his big red car to his home and office.

Among the most intriguing of the Percival Lowell legends, and one that appears to have precipitated his decision to purchase an automobile, deals with a sightseeing visit that the astronomer planned in 1909 to make to the Grand Canyon, some 80 miles distant from Flagstaff. Hiring a native driver with horses and a carriage, he left Flagstaff one spring afternoon and made camp a dozen miles northwest of town at the westerly edge of the pine and aspen-covered San Francisco peaks. The prior winter's snow had largely melted, but the fine and ubiquitous ash from the numerous volcanic cones that dot the region was still damp and at its most tedious for overland travel. Once out of the forest, the next day was slow, muddy, and tiresome going. The guide became more and more apprehensive and wanted to turn back; but Lowell was nothing if not persistent. He had paid for a visit to the canyon and insisted on completing his trip, no matter how difficult, and so they labored on until darkness again stopped their progress.

Upon awakening the following morning, Lowell found that his companion had disappeared during the night, taking with him both horses and all of Lowell's supplies. He had only what he slept in — his small tent and two blankets! Flagstaff was now more than 50 miles to the southeast, but the town of Williams was somewhat nearer and also on the railroad. So he started walking in that direction. Being an astronomer, Percival Lowell had no difficulty navigating by day or by night, but trudging across the gumbo soil of the sparsely vegetated and occasionally slushy rangeland was slow going. It was two days later when the hungry, bedraggled, muddy and momentarily penniless blue-blood arrived at the outskirts of Williams, only to find that everyone in town was fully engaged in celebrating a local holiday.

He plodded onward to the railroad depot where the station master took one look at the grubby and disheveled person standing before his wicket and refused point-blank to grant credit for the train

VII. The Motoring Lowells

Percival Lowell and members of his staff outside the Clark refractor dome. Carl Otto Lampland on right, V.M. Slipher and Wrexie Louise Leonard on steps above Lowell — 1909 (Lowell Archives).

fare back to Flagstaff. Nor would he authorize such a scruffy looking character even to send a collect telegram. In vain Lowell dropped the good name of his friend Ed Ripley, president of the Santa Fe. Completely rebuffed at the depot, the tired and increasingly ravenous scientist retreated to a local watering hole on the edge of town and again announced his identity, describing his predicament and asking if someone would please be so good as to take his word and advance the necessary funds to return him whence he belonged. Raucous guffaws greeted him on all sides — there was no way that this raggedly dressed and unshaven bum, despite his elegant manner and cultured voice, could be the real Percival Lowell that everyone had heard of. Finally, though, one roughneck flipped him a 20-dollar gold piece and told the dejected stranger that he'd take a chance on him. Thus armed with hard cash, Lowell returned to the train station and sent a telegram to his employees at Flagstaff, describing his embarrassment. Two hours later a steam engine, pulling a single car, arrived from Flagstaff, the bigger city to the east, to bear the still disheveled visitor back to his home in comfort.

That particular legend is silent as to the fate of the absconding companion and the skeptical station master, but concludes with the trusting roughneck of the saloon receiving his 20 dollars back several times over.

Lowell, however, had had enough. An avid reader, frequently of murder mysteries, he now pored through *Popular Mechanics*, *Popular Science* and other publications that dealt with various applications of the evolving internal combustion engine and its numerous producers. With the aid of his indefatigable secretary, Wrexie Louise Leonard, he communicated with several auto makers, demanding more information and details. After months of such research, and now armed with the best knowledge he could acquire, the big red car — with an especially wide rear seat to accommodate a smaller person lying full length — was ordered from the Stevens-Duryea factory in Chicopee Falls, Massachusetts. At least this carriage would not be inclined to take off without him during the night.

In making the decision to finally buy a car, Lowell went back to his New England roots, for in 1639 the first Lowell to come to America — and settle in Newbury, Massachusetts — was also named

VII. *The Motoring Lowells*

Percival. Automobile production in North America was already beginning to center in the Midwest, notably around Detroit, but the astronomer may very likely have read language similar to that appearing in a later brochure, not current in his day, which —for all of its flowery lines and irrelevant inaccuracies— was the softest and most effective of sells for a potential car purchaser of distinction and discrimination.

NEW ENGLAND CRAFTSMEN WHO
BUILD FOR THE EYES OF THE GODS

"In the elder days of Art,
Builders wrought with greatest care
Each Minute and unseen part,
For the Gods see everywhere."
Longfellow,
"The Builders"

Almost in the shadow of Mount Tom, in the foothills of the beautiful Holyoke Range, stands a factory, filled with extraordinary machines and more extraordinary men.

The Massachusetts men, and the women too, who work in this factory live in half a dozen villages— Chicopee, Chicopee Falls, Holyoke, Willimansett, Springfield. Most of them have lived here all their lives, and their families before them for many generations.

They are quiet, settled-down folk, these New Englanders, rearing families and bearing their share of civic responsibilities. They love the rock-strewn [this is a trifle fanciful, for the subsoil in all of the "villages" listed is based in glacial outwash, not the bouldery moraine that gives rise to stone walls and produces the famous New England "hard pan"] country of theirs with its stone fences and quiet farms and busy industries, though you wouldn't get them to say so unprovoked. They have traditions that date back to the Indian Wars, the expeditions against the French and the Minute Men; but they are not the sort to live on their traditions— they express them, not in words, but in their lives. They are not demonstrative, as a rule. They talk in subdued negatives—"It's not bad," they say: or "Well, it might be better."

It was the forefathers of these men who made the guns that won American Independence, who built the ships and houses and furniture, the clocks and churches and silverware that to-day we treasure, not because of their age, but for their eternal goodness and beauty and truth. They were builders who

Percival Lowell's Big Red Car

"...wrought with greatest care
Each minute and unseen part."

It is their spirit, their standards, their methods that are perpetuated to-day in the modern group of New England craftsmen. The rifles and machine guns that helped to bring victory to America and her Allies in the Great War, the fine and intricate tools and scientific instruments, the almost human machinery of modern New England, stand as witness to the loyalty of these present-day craftsmen to the ideals established by their Colonial ancestors. Faithful in workmanship, in the maintenance of self-imposed standards, in the conscious application of mind, hand and imagination, these men work for the joy of working. They do things as well as they can be done.

Nearly thirty years ago two New Englanders [if one can stretch New England ancestry to include those born in Illinois] rolled out from their little machine shop in Chicopee Falls [actually, the machine shop was in the neighboring "village" of Springfield, then boasting a population in excess of 100,000] a queer looking buggy with a one-cylinder engine in it, and set it to chug-chugging before the incredulous gaze of their neighbors. Up the village street it went, a modest announcement to the world that a new triumph was being recorded for New England inventive genius, to take its place alongside the sewing machine, the cotton gin, the telegraph, the newspaper printing press, vulcanized rubber and the discovery of electricity, for this was the first practical gasoline automobile built in America — different from any other car in the world.

A few years later America was hearing with pride of the achievements of "Duryea Motor Carriages," now brought to a high state of efficiency, in the speed and hill-climbing contests of Europe, where the best cars of England and the Continent went down to defeat before these products of Massachusetts.

The Stevens-Duryea of to-day, which is being built in this factory by the New England men, is the mature expression of the vision of the original inventors, and embodies in all respects the finest traditions of New England Craftsmanship. It is characteristically a product of New England — of New England modernized by the development of a native mechanical genius which creates for the love of creation; which, as a genuine expression of its character, builds for beauty, strength, usefulness and permanence.

In the Stevens-Duryea factory, what is known among mechanical engineers as "tolerances" are not found in working drawings and are not recognized in the processes of finishing. Absolute perfection is, of course, humanly impossible; but for Stevens-Duryea craftsmanship,

VII. The Motoring Lowells

perfection is at least set as a constant standard. In the machining of fine parts, half the fine metal is often sacrificed in order to reach the sound and flawless heart of the piece, and the final product is tested and worked over repeatedly until the limit of human accuracy has been attained.

Workmanship of such a high order is necessarily costly; but in the end it is the most economical sort, for its products endure. A Stevens-Duryea that has run two hundred and fifty thousand miles compares favorably in performance with one that has run one thousand. Its fine old engine is still quiet, still acting with precision, still capable of supreme feats of power and endurance. It is the evidence, if evidence be needed, of the worth of simplicity enforced through fine workmanship. [Every engine built by Stevens-Duryea served its "breaking in" period attached to the electric generators that powered the factory.]

Where machines can be devised that will do better and more accurate work than hands, machines are used in the Stevens-Duryea factory. Many remarkable machines, performing incredible tasks, have been designed by Stevens-Duryea engineers and machinists. Accurate as these machines are, however, no part that comes from them is passed until it has been tested and gauged in every dimension.

In all this work it is the spirit of craftsmanship that animates every brain and hand and eye. These standards of accuracy have not been imposed by Stevens-Duryea management. But by the men themselves. They were established, so far as Stevens-Duryea was concerned, nearly a generation ago. They have been upheld as a tradition, they have been practiced as a faith, they have been taught as an inspiration ever since.

They have produced a car of which the men are extremely proud. Neither New England nor America at large can ask more than that. And so long as New England craftsmen continue to make Stevens-Duryea Motor Cars, these standards will be maintained.

Big Red's First Trip

> *Almost everything still moved by railroad in those days and the Boston & Maine had spur tracks that ran through the streets of Chicopee, one of them right to the factory door. In mid–July of 1911, the now completed car was wrapped securely in all manner of blankets and tarpaulins and bundled aboard one of their flat cars for the long trip west. The factory workmen tied it down very securely and,— with a toot of the steam-engine's whistle, away the car went— west forever.*

Chicopee had been a segment of the original settlement of Springfield, back in 1636. A few years later, in 1650, when the General Court (legislature) of the Bay Colony of Massachusetts started dividing up its territory into administrative counties and townships, a group of farmers took up land along a tributary river that flowed westward into the larger Connecticut only five miles north of William Pynchon's trading post and fort. The stream was called Chicopee, after the native Narragansett Indian name for the aromatic red cedar tree, which grew in abundance along the banks of that stream. In later years, after 1820, when the power of falling water began to be harnessed all over the region, dams were built along this tributary stream, most notably at the falls near which Arthur MacArthur and his wife, Aurelia, resided. It was still a part of Springfield in 1845 when their firstborn son arrived on June 2. Arthur, Jr. became a famous military figure in American history and his son, Douglas, even more so.

VIII. Big Red's First Trip

But with the construction of the first mills in 1825, the settlement near the falls began to grow so much that the residents developed a feeling of independence from the older community centered a good hour's walk to the south. Then came the railroads, which built spur and branch lines to almost every corner of the region in the two generations after 1835 when the first line snaking inland from Boston reached a temporary terminus at Springfield on the east bank of the formidable Connecticut River. Finally, in 1848, the General Court enacted a law which set this area off as a separate legal entity from the larger township of Springfield, which now had a population of almost 11,300 persons.

The trip to Big Red's new home in Flagstaff began one morning when a Boston & Maine Railroad switching engine groaned and hissed to a stop, then coupled onto the flatcars standing on the siding next to the factory. After a few minutes of conversation between train crew and factory employees, the engine began to pull the small string down to the railroad's yards in Springfield's North End. Here Red waited until her car was attached to a freight train going north on what had been built as the Connecticut River Railroad to its junction with what had been the Fitchburg Railroad's main line until 1901, when all were consolidated — along with more than a hundred other semi-solvent New England short lines— into the Boston & Maine. When the Fitchburg line's famous tunnel under Hoosac Mountain had finally been completed in 1876, this east-west track became the principal route for freight moving in and out of the port of Boston. Though the settlements along that route were smaller and produced less way traffic, the grades via Fitchburg, Gardner and Athol were gentler than those of the competing Boston & Albany line, which ran through the larger cities of Worcester and Springfield, but then had to ascend nearly a thousand feet higher to climb over, rather than tunnel under, the crest of the Berkshire Hills to reach the West. Topping off that topographic condition, the B & A had now been leased for 999 years by the New York Central System.

It might have appeared easier on the map, at least, for Big Red's car to have been attached to a freight train going directly west from Springfield. After all, young Amasa Stone (1818–1883) and his brother-in-law, William Howe (1803–1852) had built America's first major railroad bridge there more than eighty years earlier. But, once rolling, a freight train is relatively economical to operate and maintains an enormous inertia. Thus the rates for freight and human carriage tended to be based only in part on the map distance between points A and B, not the seemingly more realistic length of trackage. Furthermore, noncompeting railroads that met at convenient junctions often combined, despite twenty years of "regulation" by the Interstate Commerce Commission, to make joint or "through" freight rates that presented an economic advantage to shippers over the use of other carriers.

Thus it was that, later in the day, when Red's flatcar was coupled into a northbound freight train, her journey westward across the continent was fairly started. The train could have made several stops on the trip north along the Connecticut River, but Red's was not a local, though it did contain a number of cars that were being sent to destinations far to the west and as well as to the north. There was no need for it to make any stops until it had gone upriver all of 35 miles to the switching yards at Cheapside in South Greenfield. But the car did travel through scenic and historic country — north through the flat farmlands of Chicopee known as Aldenville and across the Connecticut River into the larger city which had been named for Edward Augustus Holyoke (1728–1829), the American pioneer in small pox vaccination and a founder of the American Academy of Arts and Sciences.

The train rolled on upstream past the big dam across the main stream, which furnished the waterpower for a score of mills and factories in that city. Above the dam, the river was flat and tranquil for many miles, as Red's car rattled past the hard rock excavation where the bird-like fossil Tyrannosaurus footprints of Triassic Age had been quarried for exhibition in museums all over the world. The train chugged onward, traversing the fertile farmlands of the upper Pioneer Valley, which remain one of the nation's richest — if among the smallest — food producing areas. It rumbled slowly through Northampton and northward by way of more farm country in the townships of Hatfield, Whately and Deerfield, which had been names very much in the news two hundred years earlier during the French and Indian Wars. Finally, almost two hours after

VIII. Big Red's First Trip

leaving Springfield, the train wheezed to a stop in the Boston & Maine's Greenfield yards.

There was another long wait while Red's flatcar was detached from the northbound train and shunted into position to be made a part of the manifest of an incoming westbound freight whose next stop would be at the westerly end of the B & M, in New York State at Troy. Finally, the train from Boston rolled in and Red's car was attached, along with the others which the train from Springfield had dropped off at Greenfield before it picked up some more northbound cars and continued on (mostly along the river) to Brattleboro, White River Junction and eventually to Montreal.

Going west from Greenfield, the Boston & Maine tracks climbed up beside the historic Deerfield River which wound its way east from the northern Berkshire Hills down into the Connecticut. This was a turbulent little stream which drained the winter snowfall from the higher points of Massachusetts with unfettered abandon. In the days before the Army Corps of Engineers was loosed upon the American landscape with countless dam projects to control floods, generate electricity, and provide recreation — all at once — as well as spend money for political patronage, this river ran totally free and wild. As a result of its freedom, however, the little stream did what unfettered little streams always do and often rampaged down its valley during times of high runoff. This totally natural process has resulted with considerable regularity — to this day and despite the Corps of Engineers — in the removal of portions of man's intrusive railroad.

An initially greater tribulation for the railroad had been the tunnel through Hoosac Mountain to reach gentler terrain on the west side of the main range, without which it would have been unable to complete its westward extension. In 1855 the project for a tunnel had been begun, but the difficulties of the work through the complicated bedrock geology of the region soon exceeded the $1 million resources of the Troy and Greenfield Railway Company. Originally calculated to cost $1,948,557, when the four-mile tunnel was finally completed — five contractors and twenty-one years later, and after the Commonwealth of Massachusetts was forced to take over the financial burden — the project's cost had risen to more than $10,000,000. But in the end it made possible an easier and lower level route than that of the line which went more directly west from Springfield. Red's train could endure the ten minutes of smoky darkness with ease for the tunnel had almost no grade and the steam engine could now coast along without hard work. Curving northward on the west side into the southern corner of Vermont, the rails now followed down the Hoosick River and — only thirty hours after leaving Chicopee — Red was parked on a siding in the yards at Troy, on the Hudson River just across from Albany.

Because the Boston & Maine regarded the Boston & Albany as a deadly enemy, and the latter was now a captive of the much larger New York Central, the B & M's connections at Troy were with a railroad that competed with the larger system controlled by the economic heirs of Commodore Cornelius Vanderbilt, who had acquired his nautical title from his peers because of his earlier extensive interests in tug boats, ferries and other shipping that sailed in and from New York Harbor. Through a subsidiary, the Erie Railroad reached a tentacle into Troy from its main line which then ran west through the cities of Binghamton, Corning and Jamestown before connecting with another friendly railroad at Buffalo. The notorious financial peculations — some of them involving Vanderbilt — of fifty years earlier that had given the Erie line the pejorative adjective of "weary," were a thing of the past and the line was now prosperous and efficient. It did not have as direct a route as that of the Central, which largely followed the water-level line of the famous New York State Barge Canal from Albany to Buffalo. But it was scenic and enjoyed favorable rate connections with both the B & M on the east and the New York, Chicago & St. Louis Railroad — more commonly known after 1882 as the Nickel Plate Road — on the west.

And so, over the next two days, Red's flatcar was pulled over the Hudson River on the high trestle south of Albany to skirt the northern edges of the Catskill Mountains and pass well below the southern ends of New York's Finger Lakes. The tracks ran along the upper reaches of the Susquehanna River via Elmira and Hornell before reaching the more open, less hilly country south of the Great Lakes that makes up the great American Midwest.

From Buffalo westward, along the south edge of Lake Erie, the Nickel Plate tracks were at most only a few miles distant from and

VIII. Big Red's First Trip

always in direct competition with the New York Central system. In places the competitors had track-sharing agreements and in later years they were merged, shortly before the final great Northeastern railroad bankruptcy that led to Conrail. The freight from Cleveland to Chicago moved swiftly, stopping only every hundred miles or so to change crews. Along the way, Big Red passed another landmark pertinent to Amasa Stone. By 1876 he was a philanthropist of some note, Case Western Reserve University being a major beneficiary of Stone's largesse, and had become president of the Cleveland, Painesville and Ashtabula Railroad. Stone had personally designed the high iron truss bridge across Ashtabula Creek to the highest standards then known. When it collapsed on the snowy night of December 29, 80 persons were killed and Stone was so stung with remorse that he became a recluse and a few years later ended his own life. His railroad was later consolidated into the New York Central.

At Fostoria, Ohio, the freight made a much longer pause while the two segments of the train were separated and merged with other cars that had arrived earlier at this important junction. Here, Big Red had her second jolting experience with a railroad "hump." Then, one train with some of Red's companion cars for the last 400 miles took the line that turned somewhat southwest to Fort Wayne, Peoria and St. Louis while Red's and many others continued on north-westward to Chicago.

In the days when everything and everyone in America traveled by rail, it was commonly said that "a pig can cross the United States without changing cars, but everything else has to change stations in Chicago." While Red did not qualify as a pig, her flatcar did have to change railroads again, but for the final time. The Chicago Terminal Railroad, which interconnected the dozen independent lines that converged on the Windy City — almost all of them with their own separate stations for passengers — shunted her around town to the west. Here, the car was delivered to the freight yards of a famous "streak of rust" that prospered greatly during the 24-year management tenure of Boston-born Edward Payson Ripley (1845–1920) which had begun in 1896.

The Atchison, Topeka and Santa Fe Rail Railroad became known by two different names during its hundred-plus year life, before merging with and into the Burlington Northern line. To afficionados of the stock market it was always "Atchison," but to the traveling public and those who lived along its lines it was and remains the "Santa Fe," the most romantic major railroad of the American West. This was the line of Fred Harvey's famous restaurants with their decorous serving girls, the line of occasional shooting warfare with crews from General William Jackson Palmer's Denver & Rio Grande Western, and the line that everyone soon took to see the nation's greatest still-life show, the Grand Canyon. The Santa Fe of 1911 had been born of a series of mergers, of which one of the largest had been that with the Atlantic & Pacific line. Though the mergers in 1890 with the Colorado Midland and the St. Louis & San Francisco brought in more track mileage, that with the A & P brought the railroad to northern Arizona, to Flagstaff, and to the Pacific.

The Denver & Rio Grande Western, which had unsuccessfully fought for control of the Raton Pass route, did manage to retain control of the Royal Gorge passage into the mountains of western Colorado. Once using narrow (three foot) gauge for its most glamorous and exalted, but now abandoned, routes, the Rio Grande has completely disappeared from the manifest of American railroads, being absorbed first into the Southern Pacific and thence into the Union Pacific. This troublesome line was the result of merging two somewhat commonly owned lines—the Denver & Rio Grande and the Rio Grande Western. It was another romantic railroad of the American West, its scenic terrain and travails furnishing the contents of a dozen exciting books.

And so, early in August of 1911, Red's flatcar, with Lowell's automobile still bundled securely against the summer's dust, heat and showers, continued westward over the plains of northern Illinois—passing not far north of where Charles Duryea had finished his schooling—to the great cantilever bridge across the Mississippi River near its junction with the Des Moines River at Fort Madison. Crossing through the impressive trusswork, the train moved on toward the sunset through the drab but fertile wheat lands of northern Missouri to Kansas City. After a rearrangement of cars which entailed Red's final experience with a "hump," her flatcar was pulled over the Missouri River into Kansas. The main line of the Santa Fe Railroad now bypassed both Atchison and Topeka, so Red's train moved

VIII. Big Red's First Trip

rapidly across the state "of the south wind," as its earlier, red-skinned inhabitants had called the area.

Once into the equally flat terrain of southeastern Colorado the first major stop was at the Santa Fe Railroad's important and aptly named junction town of La Junta. The depredations of the James Brothers in this region were a generation in the past and there never had been much romance in holding up a freight train, so the trip was uneventful. The only hazard to traffic now encountered along this way was the occasional washout caused by the sudden flooding of a minor stream after a heavy downpour from the legendary thunderstorms of Kansas. At La Junta the train was again reconstituted, with the freight cars bound for Arizona and the Southwest being separated from those headed toward, Pueblo, Denver and the precious metal mining regions of the Colorado mountains.

To reach Arizona and the Pacific the railroad had to overcome Raton Pass before encountering the easier terrain in New Mexico leading to the line's final name city of Santa Fe. The route of the old Santa Fe pack mule and wagon trail had climbed easily up the more gentle northern approaches, but zigzagged down the south (New Mexico) side of the pass. In following the same general line, the railroad had initially used switchbacks to gain (or lose) the necessary altitude to cross the 8,560 foot pass. But, during the initial construction period in 1878, the engine of a work train had tumbled off the end of one of these arrangements and so, after "settling" one of its intermittent wars with the troublesome and fiercely independent Rio Grande line, the Santa Fe management undertook construction of a tunnel through the sandstone formations of the region to eliminate this burdensome, tedious and sometimes downright dangerous crossing. By the time that Red's train arrived at this pass, in midsummer of 1911, a second, single-tracked tunnel — slightly longer but with a grade that actually descended as the train moved west — had been opened for westbound traffic and her train moved smoothly for the three-hour trip from Trinidad on the north to Raton on the south.

It was downhill from here through the historic town of Santa Fe to join the railroad's other main stem that approached from New Orleans and other southern cities to its major junction at Belen a few miles south of Albuquerque. Once again Red's car was separated from its recent fellows and now combined with a freight that would take it to its final destination. This time, however, she was part of a local, making stops every twenty miles or so as the engine puffed its way northwestward up the long grade from the valley of the Rio Grande River to rattle by the scenic red cliffs between Grants and Gallup. Several hours after leaving Gallup, there was another crew change at Winslow in eastern Arizona just beyond the recently "discovered" region of the Petrified Forest. The country was now high, dry and bleak, with few trees. Springtime with its flowers was long gone from the desert by the time the small procession of local freight cars crossed the sandy, almost dry, bed of the Little Colorado River. After the short stop at Winslow, the train rumbled over the new bridge high above the steep-sided Canyon Diablo, and soon the extinct volcanic cones of the San Francisco Peaks—northern Arizona's landmark for all travelers— came into view. The long trip to her new home was almost ended.

Percival Lowell had established the foundation of his observatory in Flagstaff in the late spring and summer of 1894, after his agent,

A Labor Day parade moving north on Leroux Street in downtown Flagstaff— 1907 (Weatherford Hotel).

VIII. Big Red's First Trip

Andrew Ellicott Douglass, had studied the quality of "seeing" from points near such other Arizona locations as Tombstone, Tucson, Phoenix, and Prescott. He had been received with enthusiasm at all these locations, but finally settled on "a low mesa" west of Flagstaff, the eleventh site to be tested. Douglass might have done more testing, but the opposition of Mars, when the Earth's neighboring planet would be at its closest for several years, was fast approaching and his employer needed to settle on a location. When Lowell's advance man arrived in the largest settlement of northern Arizona the rail lines were still known as the Atlantic & Pacific, a corporate entity controlled by Boston financial interests. The company advertised itself in the local weekly newspaper as:

> THE GREAT MIDDLE ROUTE ACROSS
> THE AMERICAN CONTINENT
>
> In connection with the Railways of the "SANTA FE ROUTE"
> SUPERIOR FACILITIES LIBERAL MANAGEMENT PICTURESQUE SCENERY
> EXCELLENT ACCOMMODATIONS
> Observe the Ancient Indian Civilization of **Laguna,** or of **Acoma,**
> the "City of the Sky."
> Visit the **Petrified Forest** near Carrizo.
> See and marvel at the freak of **Canyon Diablo.**
> View the longest **Cantilever Bridge** in America across the Colorado river.
> From **Flagstaff** the following points of interest can easily be reached:
> The **Grand Canyon of the Colorado**, the most sublime of
> nature's work on the earth.
> The **Natural Bridge of Arizona and Montezuma's Wells**, both
> wonders to behold.
> The ruins of the pre-historic **Cave and Cliff Dwellers** will interest you.
> Take hunting trip in the magnificent forests of the
> **San Francisco** mountains.

Real news must have been slow, for almost every week during that year, Flagstaff's Coconino *Sun* ran the same lengthy piece extolling the region it served:

> ...The town is beautifully situated about seven miles southeast of the San Francisco peaks on the Colorado Plateau. It is on the main line of the Atlantic & Pacific railroad, 344 miles west of Albuquerque and

Percival Lowell's Big Red Car

834 miles from San Francisco. The business on the railroad at this point is larger than at any other station on the road between Los Angeles and Albuquerque. It is also the initial point of the Central Arizona railroad, which is intended to run to Benson via Globe, and which will pass through a fine timber and agricultural section, as yet undeveloped.

The magnificent pine forests of the county form one of the leading resources of Flagstaff. A conservative estimate by competent authorities places the stumpage at not less than 8,000,000,000 feet. Since the first saw mill was established here in 1882, the average annual cut has been about 13,000,000....

Flagstaff was to remain a lumber town for close to another 100 years, until the merchantable timber accessible from town had all been cut. But the Northern Arizona University athletes still bill themselves as "the Lumberjacks." Fortunately, at this writing the timber is now regrowing, and is largely under the management of the United States Forest Service, whose "Sustained Yield" mandate does not allow such widespread "harvesting" as was once the prevalent custom. In the same edition of the paper that announced the imminent construction of the Lowell Observatory, the editors found space for a more mundane announcement. "The strong man of the world, E. Sandow, passed through here on Saturday on No. 1, for

An eastbound local deadheads at Flagstaff's railroad station — 1892 (Lowell Archives).

VIII. Big Red's First Trip

Flagstaff's first major idustry was hauling lumber out of the woods — 1898 (Cline Library, NAU).

California, accompanied by a party of five. Three trained Shetland ponies and personal effects occupied a baggage car, which was placarded with Sandow's familiar name. It is said of Sandow, who travels on his muscle, that he can stoop down and easily lift a weight of 5,000 pounds from off the ground."

Eugene Sandow (1863–1925) was German-born but had gained a wide American fame from his appearance at the Chicago World's fair the previous year, where he was under the management of the noted Chicago-born impresario Florenz Ziegfeld.

The local newspaper may have suffered from the typical boosterism associated with many media people, but what it regularly printed about northern Arizona, where Percival Lowell's car was about to arrive, was informative and remains credibly accurate a century later. This region

> ...is celebrated for its historic associations with the ancient people who dwelt here before the discovery [by palefaces, anyhow] of America

and the cave and cliff-dwellers all of whom have left behind them interesting evidences of their peculiar character and mode of life. It is also celebrated for its enchanting scenery, mountain, cliff and vale. Here is the Grand Canyon of the Colorado, that has excited the wonder of scientific men and invoked the admiration of all beholders. Here, too, is Canyon Diablo, the painted desert, the petrified forest, the natural bridge, the bottomless pits, ancient ruins, deserted villages, around all of which, but each peculiar to itself, cluster charms and romance.

Here, too, is the great cave of the Montezuma well for visitors to marvel at, and the mineral springs of rare medicinal virtues, and a multitude of other freaks of nature that the curious make pilgrimage to see and are always rewarded for the effort.

The Grand Canyon is two hundred miles long, and at this point is eighteen miles wide and more than a mile deep, and filled with an endless variety of curiosities, massive, artistic, and beautiful, on which the eye never wearies of feasting. Then there is the mighty river pouring through the rugged cliffs, hurrying onward to its home in the sea.

In historic interest, magnificent scenery, and natural curiosity Coconino has no equal in any other part of the world. It is also noted for its healthful, buoyant climate, its rich soil and wide range of valuable productions and natural resources, a solid foundation on which to build up homes for a million or two million industrious people amid thrift, contentment and a high

The Grand Falls of the Little Colorado River, in full spate — 1913 (Lowell Archives).

VIII. Big Red's First Trip

civilization. The county is so large, exceeding in scope some of the eastern states, and so peculiarly situated with regard to physical conditions that it embraces the milder winter climate of the north and the semi-tropical of Italy. As you slip down over the mountains, to which we have referred a broad plateau of imperial proportions spreads out, having an altitude of 6,886 feet above sea level. On this plateau the climate is much like that of New York, with the absence of bleak storms in fall and winter. The snow falls a foot and a half and two feet deep and remains on the ground, firm and crisp as a rule, until it disappears in the spring.

The transition from summer to winter and winter to summer is rapid. The air at all seasons is clear, dry and bracing. The average citizen pursues his regular avocations from day to day, lives well, lays up something every year and enjoys good health. The drop from this plateau down into the Oak, Beaver and Verde valleys is abrupt, steep for five hundred feet and then gradual for one thousand feet more. In these valleys there is no cold winter, but like gentle spring, fervent summer and delightful autumn.

It is now about twelve years since the first experiment in agriculture was made on the plateau, and this with some misgivings as to the result in consequence of its altitude and other natural conditions. But the experimenter was impressed with the friendly atmosphere, the fervent sun and rich soil, and, then, he saw growing wild in abundance indigenous potatoes, peas, berries, plums, cherries, flax and hops, and he argued that where such vegetables and fruits and plants and fiber would grow wild of so excellent a character and ripen with such perfection they would still grow abundantly and of higher grade under proper cultivation, and that all the cereal would grow also. His reasoning was good and the experiment was a pronounced success. Other farmers came in, bought land, ploughed, sowed, reaped and mowed and gathered large crops years after year, demonstrating with such successive crops the perfect adaptability of this plateau region to the production of all these crops, of the best quality....

With further embellishment of the editor's ebullience for the agricultural potential of the region, the account from which the above passage was taken went on for an additional two and a half more columns, filling most of one page of the *Coconino Sun* with unfettered enthusiasm. While the agricultural aspects of this homily have yet to be substantiated, the scenery remains terrific and the big red car continues to visit almost all of it.

At Home in Flagstaff

> *Carl Otto Lampland, an astronomer on the staff described by Percival Lowell as "that spirited, noble animal," also kept a diary. When the big red car arrived on Mars Hill, Lampland became its unofficial curator and — for a while — worked at learning its foibles with almost the same fervor that he applied to his researches on the heat radiated by distant planets and stars. His diary told about the car's acclimatization problems.*

It was only a short drive from the railroad platform where Red was unloaded, west along the optimistically named Santa Fe Avenue, which was graded but unpaved and had puddles of mud left over from the afternoon thunderstorm of the day before. A few years later, much of this stretch of road beside the railway was to become part of the famous "Route 66." At the end of the city's "street" the dirt road continued north to wind up the hill and past the location at the entrance to his property where Dr. Lowell was soon to erect a lovely wrought-iron "Saturn" gate. The town had given him five acres of land when he decided to locate his observatory in Flagstaff and he had bought a lot more so as to give his telescopes the nighttime privacy that observers needed in order to use them effectively.

Those isolated summer afternoon thunderstorms often bring more noise and wind to Arizona's high plateau than they do rain. A standard feature of the "monsoon" season from mid–June to

IX. At Home in Flagstaff

Top: Mars Hill from Flagstaff in 1897, showing at center the dome housing Lowell's historic 24-inch refractor. *Bottom:* The city of Flagstaff as seen from Mars Hill—1894 (Lowell Archives).

mid–September, these storms represent the fruit of circulation around a continental high pressure area that swirls Gulf of Mexico moisture inland until southwesterly winds raise the air mass up from the lowland desert and over the 7,000-foot Mogollon Rim. The resultant adiabatic convection and cooling brings everything to the precipitation point. On their opaque, streaky pedestals of rain, these towering clouds reach to the stratosphere and march slowly across the landscape to their own crashing tympani, sometimes circling about the San Francisco Peaks until they die down with the setting of the sun to await rebirth at high noon less than 20 hours later.

As a further inducement for the Bostonian philanthropist to locate his observatory in their midst, the town fathers had also volunteered to build a "wagon road" to the top of the "low mesa" that was now called Mars Hill, after the most publicized topic of study for the largely self-taught astronomer. Some 50 yards up the hill beyond the one-time Saturn gate location, the road made a sharp turn to the left and continued up past the home of Earl Carl Slipher, the younger of the two Indiana-born brothers who also worked for Dr. Lowell on Mars Hill, and who was soon to be a leader in Arizona's "Good Roads" movement. After reaching the crest of the mesa, the road swung right, past the house occupied by the elder Slipher brother, close by the barn occupied by Venus (and her annual satellites), and on northward to a turnaround circle in front of Dr. Lowell's long, low and rambling (now 19-room) house which he called the "Baronial Mansion." A special addition had recently been built onto the west side of the house just to garage the new car and its hopefully permanent caretaker.

Percival Lowell was born in Boston on March 13, 1855, the son of Augustus and Katherine (Lawrence) Lowell. His family was distinguished in the business and philanthropic life of New England — his maternal grandfather had been an erudite and welcome ambassador to England and another ancestor was the founder of Boston's famous Lowell Institute (later to be a major contributor to America's public television

Percival Lowell held by his mother, Katherine — 1855 (Lowell Archives).

IX. At Home in Flagstaff

system). An illustrious antecedent named John Lowell had been among the first federal judges appointed by George Washington, and a nearer relative of the same name was soon to be appointed by Abraham Lincoln; there was also a cousin and soon-to-be Civil War cavalry general "Beau Sabreur," Charles Russell Lowell, for whom the fort built to intimidate Apaches in southern Arizona was later named, and that worthy's brother, James, on his way to world-wide recognition as a poet/philosopher.

Young Percy became an honors graduate from Harvard College in 1876, where he was such a brilliant, Phi Beta Kappa student of mathematics that he was asked to assume a faculty position upon graduation. Instead, after leaving college, he opted to work for his grandfather, John Amory Lowell, at the family's Appleton Mills along the Merrimack River in the northern Massachusetts city which bore the family name. Interested from early childhood in travel, as well as the study of astronomy—for which mathematical competence is essential—in 1883, a year after the death of his grandfather, the young man gave up the business world first for a life of public service and then for greater fame in the pursuit of scientific knowledge.

Percival Lowell then absented himself to the Far East, where he lived for the next several years, learning the Japanese language and culture while making frequent visits to the supposedly independent but still Japanese-dominated land of Chosen (modern Korea). Early during his sojourn in the Far East, he took time out to serve as secretary and escort for a Korean trade delegation visiting the United States, even taking them to the White House to meet with President Chester Alan Arthur. Well over a century after Lowell's visit to Japan's Inland Sea peninsula of Noto, the natives of that region still regard him with respect for his literary work on their "Unexplored Corner of Japan." After writing numerous articles for the *Atlantic Monthly* and other comparable publications and compiling three books on Japan and Korea, in 1893 Lowell returned to the United States, now determined to pursue the serious study of astronomy, concentrating initially on the planet Mars, the most visible neighbor and frequently nearest to Earth in the solar system.

He began as an enthusiastic admirer of Virginio Schiaparelli, the noted Milanese astronomer whose concentration on the nearest

Top: North side view of Lowell's "Baronial Mansion" in 1909, before Big Red's garage was added. *Right:* Percival Lowell with members of the Korean trade mission to America—1883 (Lowell Archives).

planet, Mars, had brought him to the belief that there were inexplicable linear markings on its surface. In those days before photography had been effectively applied to astronomical pursuits, observers of the heavens sketched their findings in longhand, while peering through the eyepieces of their telescopes. It was an inexact method, at best, but all there was at the time. Lowell drew many sketches of Mars, then traced his findings onto small globes. He then entered into a long correspondence—almost entirely in their common language of French—with

IX. At Home in Flagstaff

Schiaparelli at his Brera Observatory near the center of modern Milan. The older man's eyesight was deteriorating, and his mantle of authority on these "canali" soon passed to the younger enthusiast, though his communications to Lowell occasionally took on elements of caution not to "see" things that could not be well verified by the observations of others.

Lowell, whose academic training was also in physics, the scientific corollary to mathematics, was to receive honorary degrees from both Amherst College and Clark University as a tribute to his scientific work. In addition to popularizing the possibility of some form of intelligent life having once existed on the red planet, in 1902 Lowell postulated the further possibility of there being a ninth significant member of the solar system out there in the cold beyond Neptune. He based this prediction on the anomalies in the orbit of Uranus which were not explained by the discovery of Neptune. His subsequently enormous mathematical labors in determining the existence of a "Trans-Neptunian planet" were summarized in a 1915 treatise bearing that title, and published the year before his death. But it was not until a dozen years later, after settlement of the lengthy litigation surrounding his will, that the people of Lowell's observatory were able to begin an effective search for his "Planet X."

Lowell's sketches of Mars, showing the "canali" and polar icecaps — 1907 (Lowell's Archives).

The success of that program was announced on the seventy-fifth anniversary of Percival's birth, March 13, 1930, after the completion of a gift from Percival's one-year-younger brother, Abbott Lawrence Lowell, then president of Harvard University. He had provided the funding necessary for the completion and installation of a wide-area astrograph — essentially a camera capable of taking hour-long, 14 by 18 inch pictures with a super telephoto lens. Dr. Vesto Melvin Slipher (almost always known simply as "V.M.") the older brother of "E.C."

Lowell (fourth from left) in his Tokyo garden, with three American friends and Miyaoka—1892 (Lowell Archives).

and now director of the observatory, provided a plan of search based on Lowell's calculations. Within a few nights of starting to work in 1930, a series of photographs taken early in the year by V.M.'s young assistant, Clyde Tombaugh, provided proof of the existence of what was soon named "Pluto," after the Roman god of the cold and distant regions of the "underworld." The discovery was smaller than Lowell had predicted, and with a more elliptical orbit—but it was where he had said it could be found. It was more than a coincidence then that the combined letters "P" and "L" form the classical shorthand for the name of the god, the astronomical shorthand for that of the planet, and the initials of Percival Lowell.

Proof of the existence of Lowell's "Planet X" was greeted as a remarkable scientific event as well as a posthumous vindication of

IX. At Home in Flagstaff

his greatest personal work. But the planet was considerably smaller than expected, with a more elliptical orbit that was also inclined much more than other members of the solar system to the "invariable" plane of the sun's equator. Some astronomers felt, then and later, that it was hardly a planet worthy of the name. But further study proved that it had a spherical shape, an atmosphere, a satellite and a rotational period (day). These conditions make Pluto at least two up on Mercury and one ahead of Venus, which have been happily accepted as planets since the beginning of astronomy. One of the worst difficulties that the "reformers" had in trying to denigrate Pluto from its planetary status was that no one had ever defined what a planet was—thus it was even more difficult to decide what was not.

Further and more recent studies conducted at Lowell Observatory indicate that the difference between Lowell's calculations regarding his "Planet X" and what Pluto turned out to be may be explained by the existence, documented by several later Lowell Observatory scientists, of many hundreds, perhaps thousands, more "Kuiper Belt" objects out in the dark and cold regions beyond the orbit of the Sun's ninth planet.

The search for Pluto, however, had an interesting additional result. Thanks to focusing initially on the likeliest locations in which to look, as given in Lowell's memoir, the planet was located very early in the search. But the project of compiling a full inventory of the heavens down to the sixteenth magnitude was continued to include all of the sky readily visible from Flagstaff. When Henry Lee Giclas reviewed the results a quarter century later, he repeated the original plates and thereby determined the proper motions for countless distant stars and galaxies. This "second effort" resulted in a reference work that is a "must" for any astronomical library.

While continuing his observational studies of Mars, Dr. Lowell was frequently visited by other dignitaries and scientists from all over the world. He would take his visitors on sightseeing trips around northern Arizona, to such interesting and scenic locations as Oak Creek, Turkey Tanks, Meteor Crater, Grand Canyon, Strawberry Crater, Walnut Canyon, Grand Falls, Sunset Crater, Wupatki Ruins and others. During these trips, Lowell, a renaissance scientist, frequently made botanical analyses, reporting them to his academic

associates at Harvard's Arnold Arboretum. This process resulted in the identification of several new species now bearing his name. But, as time went by, the tedium of travel by horse-drawn carriage on these ventures became increasingly unattractive as the horseless carriage evolved into greater reliability and came into ever more popular usage. Indeed the evolution of such vehicles was at first hailed as a great reducer of pollution. Statistics citing the millions of tons of horse manure and gallons of horse urine expelled onto the streets of New York City alone during the course of the year (not to mention the 17,000 horse cadavers) were impressive convincers that the burning of unpredictable amounts of gasoline might be preferable.

Top: Henry Giclas, at age thirty-seven, cleaning the "Pluto" telescope—1947. ***Bottom:*** At the Sunset Crater Aa lava flow — 2000 (Lowell Archives).

After its appearance in Flagstaff, the big red car's first long journey under its own power had to be postponed for two weeks, because — like most other recently arrived, first-time visitors to Flagstaff — she immediately began to have trouble with the altitude. At seven thousand feet above sea-level, the dry and clear surroundings of Arizona's high plateau were then, and remain still, a great place for astronomers to study the heavens. But almost a quarter of the Earth's atmosphere

IX. At Home in Flagstaff

is below that altitude and this condition was considerably different from that which the Stevens-Duryea people, back nearer sea-level in Chicopee had designed their carburetors to cope with. People and other living creatures soon adapt to thinner air by generating an increase in red blood corpuscles—the oxygen-carrying cells. But internal combustion engines have no such internal and self-compensating system. If she had been a mountain climber, Big Red's most fundamental ailment would have been diagnosed broadly as altitude sickness. The diary of Carl Otto Lampland the astronomer who became the car's unofficial caretaker, reported several problems:

Top: Cresting Sedona's Schnebly Hill — 2000. *Bottom:* Lowell's big red car at the Heiser ruins — 2000.

Aug. 27 • Tried to help Costello with the car. It is not working well.

Sept. 2 • Car gave trouble about noon on returning to town. Dr. L. and I got part way up hill. Costello and I spent afternoon locating the trouble. Gears of the [water] pump ruined by fan shaft sticking fast due to pieces of lead getting in. Rained on us.

Sept. 4 • Mr. Clark from Los Angeles arrived this evening [by train] to repair car. He began work about 8:30 P.M. and continued until 3:00 A.M. Pump gears were put in, clutch removed, cam motion adjusted, etc.

Sept. 5 • Mr. Clark resumed work on motor car and it was ready for work before noon. Took a run to the village and back. In the afternoon, Sykes [Stanley, the machinist] went out for lessons. Dr. Lowell and Mrs. L. also drove. Several candidates for drivers for the White Mountain trip. Spent most of the day with the car — "joy rides." Evening ... took Mr. Clark around to the domes.

Sept. 6 • Sykes and Costello busy getting the car and accessories ready for the expedition to the White Mountains.

Twenty years later, Stanley Sykes, the erudite English-born instrument-maker employed at Lowell Observatory from its founding in 1894 until his death in 1955, related the story of that week-long trip to Arizona's White Mountains which began on September 7. His continuous good humor and sophisticated dry wit endeared him to every visitor, and he became a favorite associate of the observatory's founder and subsequent proprietors who all took great pleasure in visiting the machine shop presided over by such a delightful gentleman.

> The automobile with all the camping gear in place was loaded on a flat car at the freight depot in Flagstaff on September 7 and shipped off to Holbrook, eighty miles away. Dr. Lowell, Judge E.M. Doe, a good friend of Lowell's [who later represented Lowell's widow in trying to break his "good friend's" will], myself [whose older brother, Godfrey, also worked several years at the observatory] and Costello, the chauffeur, took a passenger train to Holbrook, then proceeded south with the car on what is now State Route 77, following near the railroad's Apache Branch toward the White Mountains.
> The car was really loaded with camping gear. Tents and boxes of food were strapped to the running boards. Frying pans, pots, and loaves of bread dangled from the folded-down top. It made quite an impression and was a real excitement for the residents of the small Mormon villages we drove through. We camped at Cooley's ranch a spell, and then a couple of nights at Horseshoe Cienaga at the end of the Mogollon Rim, some twenty miles west of the present [but then nonexistent] town of McNary. The roads were not much, but there was some logging starting in the area and we managed to get around a good bit on some of their roads.
> Judge Doe did not like to sleep on the ground in a tent, like the rest of us; so he slept sitting up in the back seat of the car wrapped in a

IX. At Home in Flagstaff

bearskin robe with a bottle of bourbon placed between his feet. Every time he woke up, he would take a healthy snort from the bottle and then go back to sleep. The bearskin robes must have been a regular accouterment of the big red car as, many years later, they were discovered in a box in the Baronial Mansion basement. Some of the astronomers used them to keep warm when observing at the 13-inch [Pluto] telescope.

Sykes went on to describe how, on this trip, he verified for himself that Percival Lowell really did have extremely keen eyesight. Lowell was able to tell the other passengers that a windmill was turning at a farm house down the road, long before any of them could even discern that there was a windmill. He could also discern the steeple on a church building in one of the little towns long before anyone else could make it out. In the closed company of astronomy, there were many skeptics about what Lowell kept reporting concerning the changing nature of "canals" on Mars—lines that more modern

Percival Lowell at the doorway of his home surrounded by staff and servants—1905 (Lowell Archive's).

methods have shown to mark changes in the albedo of the planetary surface. Since the red planet is subject to frequent dust storms, when the atmosphere subsequently clears, these lines have often changed — a process that gave rise to multiple and frequently contradictory descriptions of these features of the Martian surface.

Lowell, largely self-educated in astronomy but persistent as an observer, was among the small minority of observers who felt they were actually seeing something real in these markings. This was the line of scientific conjecture begun a generation earlier by the celebrated Milanese astronomer Virginio Schiaparelli. After Lowell succeeded to the Italian's research mantle, his persistent study gave him reason to theorize on the whats and whys of these lines. He attributed them to the desperate work of a race of water-dependent beings, trying to eke out their livelihoods on an increasingly dry planet whose mass, and hence gravitational attraction, was ever less sufficient to retain the available moisture.

As all of the sun's satellites orbit their parent star, some parts of their atmospheres — the lightest and highest — are continually being left behind, while new matter is being intercepted and acquired. If any planet has sufficient mass and hence gravitational attraction, as do Earth and Venus, the net of this process is stability. Mars, on the other hand, is smaller and thus not quite so retentive of its lighter elements. To Lowell, these Martian "canals" seemed like huge public works projects that intelligent beings had constructed to draw the remaining water from the obvious polar icecaps of Mars toward the planet's equatorial regions, the only places where food could be grown in the much chillier climate of a celestial body with a lesser atmosphere, a notably more elliptical orbit and always farther away from the warmth of our common parent, the sun.

Percival Lowell was not afraid to speak out. His intriguing theories made good copy and his lecture tours were frequent, all of which gave rise to a lot of later science fiction, starting with that of Herbert George Wells. To quite a few of his scientific peers, on the other hand, Percival Lowell was a dangerous amateur and possibly a crackpot. However, his massively saving grace was that he spent his own money in the pursuit of knowledge and never sought aid from the public trough or panhandled others to help support his work.

IX. At Home in Flagstaff

Percival Lowell put all his assets, both in life and death, where his mouth had been, and modern science has established that on the major theses that he espoused, he was right. Generations after his death, life of some sort has been proven to have existed on Mars; there was, indeed, a ninth planet — possibly thousands more; and that look into "spiral nebulae" has led to the foundation of all modern cosmology.

On the second of these counts, the late, great, scientific enunciator, Carl Edward Sagan, came to Flagstaff in 1994, a few years before his death, to deliver a speech on the occasion of Lowell Observatory's centennial. His closing comment, after discussing the evolution of scientific knowledge over the previous hundred years, was: "When the first of America's astronauts reaches the planet, Mars — and some day they surely will — their first act should be to erect a statue to the memory and honor of Percival Lowell."

On their way home from the White Mountains, somewhat south of the hamlet of Snowflake, the road became very muddy and the car lost traction and got stuck, motionless. Sykes walked to the nearest farmhouse and hired the farmer to bring his team of horses to pull them out of the mud and around the flooded section of the road. What they found after reaching safety again was that, several days earlier, the relatively narrow wheels of the heavily laden car had cut into the raised bank of an irrigation ditch where it crossed the road. Water had then trickled down the unpaved roadway for three days, soaking it thoroughly. This was only the first instance of using two real horses' power to move Big Red's forty useless ones through some otherwise impassable situation; but it was a frequently encountered condition and gave rise to a rescue procedure that her owners and drivers were to make frequent use of.

This was a much different country from that whence Big Red had come. Not only was the altitude a problem, but the average annual precipitation in Chicopee was about 45 inches while that of Flagstaff was less than half as much, with close to half of that coming as midsummer "gully-washers." Almost everything about Arizona's high plateau is thus vastly different from southern New England. In all of Coconino County's 18,573 square miles, there were only some 8,000 souls, whereas in the city of Chicopee's 20 square miles, there

A tour out on the reservation. Big Red's left front wheel is in the foreground — 1914 (Lowell Archives).

IX. At Home in Flagstaff

were close of 40,000. In the whole state of Arizona — then the nation's fifth largest in area — there were $21 million in bank deposits, with a loan to deposit ratio of 70 percent. That was far less favorable than in Chicopee's Hampden County alone. However, by the time Big Red left Arizona in 1938, the state had more than $91 million in bank deposits and a loan to deposit ratio of 40.3 — which compared very favorably with that of Hampden County, back in Massachusetts. Thanks to the likes of Percival Lowell, the nation's economic center of gravity was moving westward, though not nearly as fast as the nation's population.

A different chauffeur-mechanic, also named Louis, appeared on the scene when Dr. and Mrs. Lowell returned from a visit to Phoenix on September 21. Apparently he felt that his duties were to be solely with the new automobile and when he was put to work painting the canvas covering of a new dome that housed what had briefly been the world's largest Newtonian focus reflector*— his stay on Mars Hill became shortened measurably. Before the end of the month Louis was gone. Another short-lived replacement was briefly on the scene for the first week of October, but he didn't measure up and was gone before another week was out. Then came Gormley, who — after his initial difficulties — was to stay with the big red car considerably longer. Lampland recorded the sequence:

Sept. 22 • Helped Louis with the automobile.

Sept. 23 • Went out with the chauffeur to see him drive. E.C.S and I went out toward mountain. Afterwards I went out the same way with Bishop [Isaac Morton] Atwood [the 74-year-old Universalist theologian, writer and administrator of Boston].

---

*All reflecting telescopes use a system of bouncing the light from the primary mirror to a secondary mirror lodged back up in the telescope tube. Newtonian focus telescopes — named for Sir Isaac Newton (1642–1727) — are now rare, for the secondary mirror was placed at a 45° angle to bounce the light out of the telescope, at a point high above the floor of the dome. Most modern telescopes use the "Cassegrain" — named for an obscure 17th century French inventor — system of bouncing the light back down through a hole in the primary mirror to a point safely below. Astronomers have been known to be seriously injured in falls from the Newtonian focus observation point; not so from the Cassegrain.

Sept. 24 • A very pleasant day. Dr. Lowell very kindly offered to let us take the machine for a trip to the mountains. Went out the mountain road and on the Tuba [City] road to a point where a superb view is had of the Painted Desert.

Sept. 25 • Work on auto with Louis. Also got him started on painting the 40" dome.

Sept. 30 • Louis is no more; the irrepressible "authoratic" of the automobile.
New chauffeur taking up the work. Louis here again with his tale of woe.

Oct. 1 • Le Ray the new chauffeur. Took us out toward Turkey Tanks [an archeological site and perennial water hole a dozen miles east of Flagstaff]. Very beautiful country.

Oct. 8 • Sunday. In the afternoon went for an auto ride to Turkey Tanks. The new driver is here and he certainly knows the business.

Oct. 12 • Dr. Lowell, Mrs. L, ECS and Gormley [new chauffeur] made a trip with auto and horses to the Peaks [the San Francisco Peaks dominate the north skyline from Flagstaff].

Oct. 18 • Gormley feeling poorly. Dr. says appendicitis.

Oct. 26 • Gormley left for hospital at Albuquerque.

Nov. 1 • New chauffeur began work [Robert Norton].

Dec. 4 • In afternoon helped Gormley replace pump gear in auto.

Dec. 6 • In afternoon helped Gormley on car. All done by 3:00 P.M.

Dec. 12 • Gormley left this evening.

Dec. 17 • Norton's last day on work. The auto went wrong this morning. It had to be pulled up the hill by block and tackle. We were quite fortunate to get this work done before the snow got too deep. The job took about all afternoon.

1912

Jan. 14 • Spent about all day on auto—realigning drive shaft and adjustment of gear change.

IX. At Home in Flagstaff

Jan. 15 • In the evening took the auto out. Had a jolly time making the hill. The dash pot in the carburetor had become loose.

Jan. 18 • Took the car out for a spin this evening. It did not work well. The carburetor is apparently all out.

Jan. 20 • Worked on auto this afternoon—carburetor. Had trouble getting up the hill. It is evident that the compression is at fault. Adjusted carburetor as nearly as possible according to directions.

Jan. 21 • Sunday. Spent most of the day on auto. Finally succeeded in getting it into good condition. Went out to the reservoir [north of town toward the Grand Canyon] and Greenlaw's [a sawmill one mile east of town]. Worked on improving compression — dissolving carbon with kerosene, took out the spark plugs, poured kerosene into cylinders, turned valves in their seats.

Feb. 1 • Put in 12 to 2 P.M. on car. Removed spark plugs, poured kerosene into cylinders, turned valves, etc.

Feb. 2 • Went out to Garings [dairy at Dry Lake, three miles west of Flagstaff] with car this afternoon—Mrs. L. and ELW [Elizabeth Williams, Lowell's principal mathematical assistant], Mrs. Doe [wife of judge], Curtis [Frank C., an assistant instrument maker], and myself. Everything went well.

Feb. 6 • Wired to Stromberg for carburetor.

Feb. 7 • Getting auto ready for Mrs. Lowell and took her to the village at 2 P.M. and again at about 5:30 P.M.

Feb. 8 • Dr. & Mrs. Lowell and Mr. Worthington [an occasional observer and assistant] left for Chicago this morning. Took them to the station in auto and everything went well. Went to the village in auto during the forenoon to attend to errands.

Feb. 10 • Replaced casings of rear wheels of auto from 3 to 6 P.M. Also removed carburetor and looked over new one for fitting, etc. (New carburetor arrived this P.M.).

Feb. 11 • Sunday. Spent most of day on the auto. Planned fitting of new carburetor and replacing old one. During P.M. went for an auto ride. VMS [Vesto Melvin Slipher was just completing his monumental spectrographic study that determined the expansion of the universe], ECS, Marcia [daughter of V.M.], and Verna [Mrs. Lampland]. In the village we picked up three young ladies and gave them a ride out to Greenlaws and Lockets [tract of land three miles east of Flagstaff]. Machine worked well.

Gormley was the last of the specially hired chauffeur/mechanics. He never returned from his appendicitis operation and his place as custodian of the big red car was effectively taken over by Lampland, with occasional assists from Stanley Sykes and his son, Harold. But Big Red's altitude adjustment problems were still far from over. One month later, on March 4, the day that William Howard Taft began his last year in office as president of the United States, Wrexie Louise Leonard, Lowell's loyal and longtime secretary, wrote Lampland from Boston: "I hope the weather will permit of your motoring Mr. Young — my cousin — to the cliffs while he is there. Dr. Lowell tells me you are an excellent chauffeur. That red car must look rather stunning out in the desert...."

Ten feet of snow fell around year-end 1915 and collapsed the roof of the Emporium Theater (Weatherford Collection, NAU).

IX. At Home in Flagstaff

But Lampland was still far from happy with Big Red's "asthma." Not only had he been in communication with the Stromberg people about their carburetor, but he had been vocal in his complaints to the factory back in Chicopee. His employer was in Europe on one of his periodic trips, for which he preferred — as did a great many upper crust Americans — to travel on one of the North German Lloyd vessels. On this occasion it was the *Auguste Victoria* on which he was accompanied by the president of Amherst College, from whose institution he had recently received an honorary doctorate (his second such tribute). On 20 April, with Dr. Lowell not due back from for another two weeks, Lampland fired back a note to Wrexie in which he reported on his activities with the Stevens-Duryea Company's pacifier, a gentleman named William Bowman, who had originally been employed as a drop forger, but was now a traveling troubleshooter.

> I asked him to send us a new carburetor, the best one he can find. Several chauffeurs tinkered with the old one and they did not seem to accomplish anything with it. Even if it could be made to work better than it has in the past, it is going to take time to locate its ailments — and it is time we are short of. You might impress on him that it will be good for his own welfare and peace of mind to send me a good carburetor! The original one can be returned to him, and he can overhaul it and put it in another car, or put the parts in stock as extras. I have had a Stromberg carburetor on trial and the two short trips made with it show a much greater mileage to the gallon than the original carburetor. Where gasoline sells at 28–30¢ any wasteful use of it will soon amount to the price of a carburetor, as the best ones can be bought for $35–$40. As you will see from my letter, I have written Bowman that the Stromberg gives better results than the Stevens, but that I am returning it with the expectation that he will send another Stevens.
>
> It will surely be a relief to get the Halley's Comet stuff out of the way, as we hope it will be before long. Evidently other observatories are finding the old comet laborious too, for no large memoirs have appeared yet.
>
> How is the weather in New England by this time? We are living in hopes that spring will be here before long....

But by 3 July, things had taken a decided turn for the better. Lampland wrote a two-page letter to his employer:

Percival Lowell's Big Red Car

Dear Dr. Lowell:

It seems to me the car works more beautifully every time I take it out. It is difficult for me to imagine how a machine could perform better. It has steadily improved these past months. The gasoline consumption per mile is now much less than at the time the report was sent to Mr. Bowman. The car had been driven by Costello, "Louis," Robert and Gormley. The gasoline used and the mileage then stood at about 300 gallons for 1064 miles—about 3½ miles per gallon. I heard you say to the chauffeurs again and again that they were using too much "oil" and it turns out that you were entirely right. At that time I did not know anything about carburetor adjustments and supposed, of course, that experienced men like Clark and Gormley should have been able to find the most perfect adjustments. After driving the car a few times I began to look into the matter and kept an accurate account of the gasoline used and the mileage. After a short time I could get better than 5 miles per gallon, and a little later this was increased to 6 and 7 miles per gallon....

Mr. Bowman has asked if the extra parts sent with the car could be returned. I wrote him that this matter would have to be referred to you. I should advise you to keep these in your possession until the car account is settled. It would remove a temptation to credit the extras returned on the account of the new parts sent out this spring!

I think there are a few other points I should mention, but they have escaped me just for the moment. I shall have to go down and see a little "broncho busting" this evening. It is a cruel sport and I care very little for it. Flagstaff celebrates two days this year....

Cruelty notwithstanding, there were other compensations in what remained of America's Wild West. In 1915, Percival's nephew Roger Lowell Putnam, who was later to serve as trustee of the Lowell Observatory for forty years, graduated from college and decided to drive across the country — visiting his famous uncle en route. Tire changes and mechanical difficulties beset him and his companion repeatedly on the dusty trip westward from Boston, but after crossing the last serious obstacle, the Little Colorado River, they were heartened by the down-home, frontier reality that greeted them upon their entry within the city limits of Flagstaff. On the first eating house they saw was a sign advertising "Meals—25¢; Good Square Meals—50¢; Reg'lar Gorge—$1.00

HIGHWAYS

The Romans had built roads that were better than most of those to be found in North America. Their Via Flaminia and Via Appia can still be traversed, if a trifle bumpily after 2000 years of use and neglect. But in the United States, such famous lines — a fraction of their age — as the "Oregon Trail" can no longer even be identified for most of their length.

In 1911, highways were a true rarity in a territory as large as Arizona but with barely a thousand motor vehicles. The first organized "intercity" highway in America had been the original Boston Post Road, which was laid out and built by order of Governor Francis Lovelace of New York in 1672, to carry the royal mails between New York and Boston. With a number of major modifications this later became the busiest part of U.S. #1. More than a century later, in 1794, the Lancaster Turnpike, running west from Philadelphia some 65 miles to Lancaster, became the first major inter-city highway in America to be paved using the system only recently evolved by the visiting Scots-born engineer John MacAdam. Thereafter began a boom in carriage and wagon road–building in the United States. Many states chartered privately owned and built turnpikes, so named because of the "pike" that one had to turn in order to pay for and gain entry to the "highway." In New Hampshire, all the famous "notches" in the White Mountains were soon traversed by such roadways—though originally passable only for horseback transit. In Massachusetts, the publicly financed "turnpike" beginning in East Boston and running some 30 miles to downtown Newburyport, was absolutely straight — over hill and dale, river and pond, through fen and forest — all the way.

Plank roads had enjoyed a brief period of popularity because of their initial smoothness and the lesser requirement for roadbed preparation in wet areas. The first of such roads was built through part of the swampy Russian capital of St. Petersburg in 1820 and another across a stretch of muskeg near Toronto in 1835. In the United States, a plank road was built for a record 16 miles from Syracuse northwest to Lake Oneida in 1846. These roads were delightfully smooth for their initial year or two. Thereafter, they became increasingly less so, verging finally into the lethal. A bumpier but longer-lived relative of the plank road in swampy regions was that constructed of "corduroy" — bare logs, laid closely together transverse to the direction of the road, and so named because of their collective ribbed appearance — similar to the cotton cloth that was made for French royalty, hence "*cord du roi.*"

In 1811, the first federal highway funding in the United States made possible the "Great National Road" from Cumberland, Maryland, to Wheeling, Virginia (the separate state of West Virginia did not come into existence until 1863). Eventually extended to St. Louis, this became the most popular land route for settlers in Conestoga (and other) wagons moving from the coast to the interior of the country prior to the growth of railroads a generation later. Across the Mississippi, the Santa Fe Trail had first been prospected in 1821 by the 33-year-old trader William Becknell from Independence, Missouri, westward, mostly along the watershed just north of the Arkansas River to its name location in the New Mexico Territory. It was progressively improved over the next two generations until it was finally superseded in 1880 by completion of the Santa Fe Railroad. This line of travel was well used by stagecoaches and had been the scene of a number of robberies and Indian attacks.

Flagstaff citizens were active in the effort to make better roads, both privately, as in the Good Roads Association, and publicly. As early as 1894, David Babbitt was asked by his fellow County supervisors to make representations on the part of Coconino County for

X. Highways

the need to expand and improve communications within the territory. He was the eldest of the five brothers who arrived in town in 1886 carving out a ranching, merchandizing and real estate empire for their descendants, most of whom are still prominent in the local political, social and economic structure, and even onto the state and national scenes.

Telephone service had begun in Flagstaff in 1886, initially between selected outposts of the Riordan's lumber mill, the town's principal employer. Communications needs took a great leap forward after 1900 when the territory's "normal" school, now Northern Arizona University, home of the Lumberjacks, was established in town. A decade after Percival Lowell had established his observatory in 1894, the Summit Telephone Company was organized and began running its lines through town. It provided service to all of 51

Winter snowstorms can be a big event on Arizona's High Plateau, particularly on Mars Hill —1935 (Lowell Archives).

subscribers by the fall of 1905, but there was no published directory, so everyone's number was printed in the local newspaper. With such a limited base of subscribers, that first company soon went broke, but its system was taken over by another with greater optimism and finally, in 1909, the Arizona Overland Telephone Company began operations in the city of Flagstaff. The next year, it offered 24-hour service and adventurous folk could even make calls to points as far distant as Phoenix. Lowell's observatory, where the most urgent communications need was for a telegraphic connection with the Naval Observatory in Washington to get its daily time check, was slow to subscribe. Mars Hill had been connected to the world by telegraph since 1894 and finally signed up for a telephone — as well as a car — in 1911. It was Number 129.

Meantime, back in Springfield, events — or at least the local congressman — had taken a wrong turn. Fifty-two-year-old Frederick

Looking east on Flagstaff's Santa Fe Avenue —1911 (Lowell Archives).

X. Highways

Huntington Gillett, who represented the 2nd District of Massachusetts from 1893 to 1925, had acquired one of the Stevens-Duryea Company's first models. After all, he claimed to be a Progressive Republican. On the morning of July 31, 1903, he was driving eastward towards Boston with one of his more important constituents, the treasurer of the Chapman Valve Company. Mr. Gillett found the roadway so rough that he attempted to drive part way up a minor local eminence named Stony Hill with the left wheels of his car on the roadbed of the adjacent trolley line company. It didn't work. Seeing a bit of washout in the trolley line roadbed, he attempted to turn back onto the "highway," but the strain of hitting the rails was too much for the left front wheel and the axle snapped, throwing the congressman out of the car, over the dashboard and onto the pavement. He was knocked unconscious, but was quickly given medical care and made a full recovery. Sixteen years afterwards, Gillett was elected Speaker of the House and later U.S. Senator.

In all of the Arizona Territory that year there were only some 210,000 people, natives included — a density of 1.9 per square mile, with considerably more males than females (a ratio that did not change until 1970). There were no buses at all, about 40 trucks, and only 1150 passenger cars in the whole territory, resulting in a ratio of 176 persons per vehicle. This was considerably lower than the national average; the West was still largely on horseback. The population of the United States remained concentrated in the Northeast, as did the bulk of the nation's 618,727 motorized vehicles. As a territory Arizona had no automobile registrations, a process that began with statehood the following year, but the territorial legislature in its final year of existence had appropriated some $2 million for road construction. Dr. Lowell's 1915 registration certificate for his big red car has survived, as well as the handwritten entry into the state's tax rolls. They both bear the number 1871; 700 new vehicles had arrived since 1911.

Agitation was growing for a Federal Highway System in the summer of 1911, but nothing much had been done at the time Big Red arrived in the unpaved lumber and cow town of Flagstaff. Outside of major cities, there were only some 2.3 million miles of public roads in the entire nation, most of them unpaved. Quite a bit of ferment — largely in the Northeast and a generation earlier — had arisen among

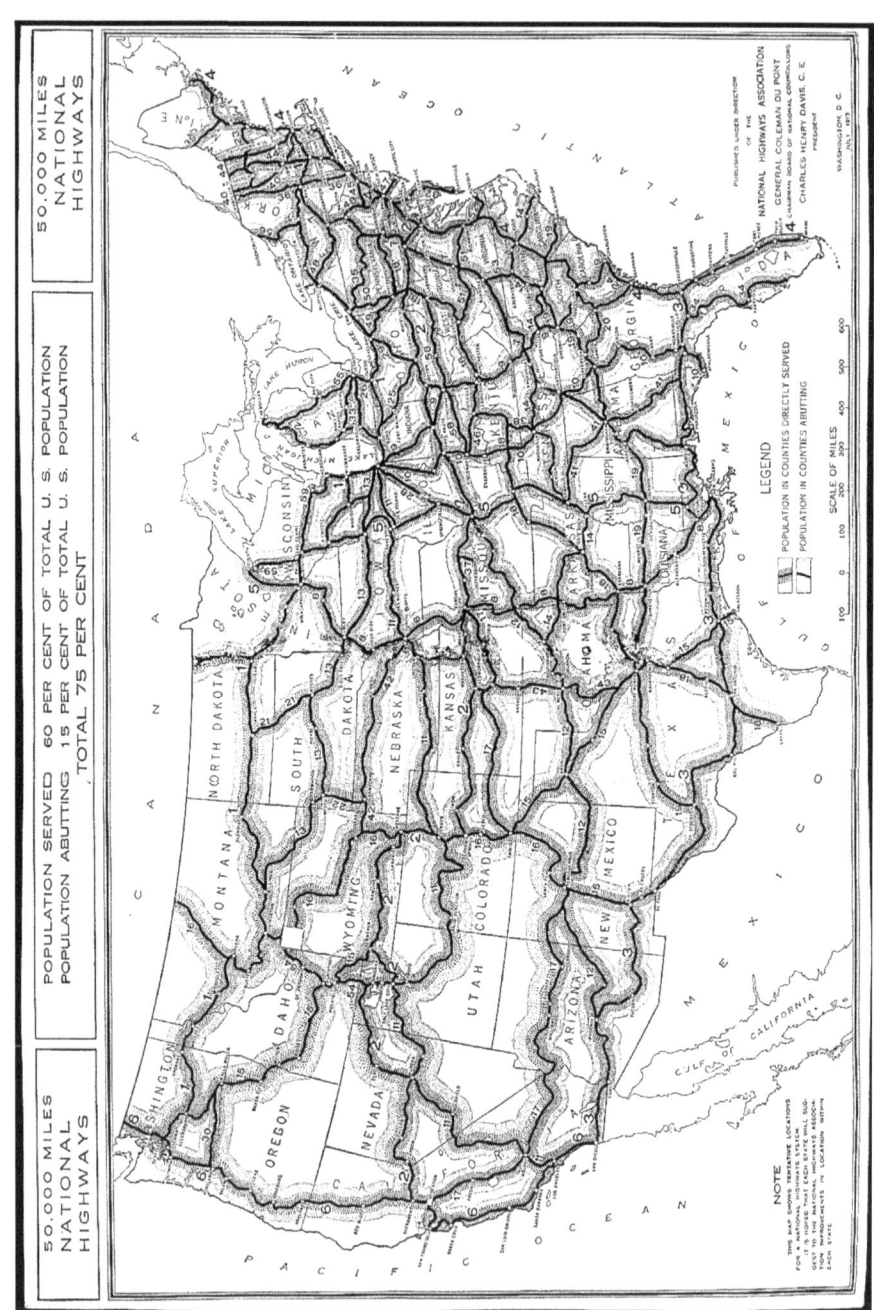

X. Highways

bicyclists agitating for better roads, but that was before a good many of such people became motorized. Finally, in 1912, after years of increasingly intense lobbying by automobile interests, Congress got around to appropriating half a million dollars to study the issue. The following year, a group under the aegis of industrialist and politician Thomas Coleman Du Pont (1863–1930), a sometime general, and retired admiral Charles Henry Davis (1845–1927), an authority on navigation, came into being calling itself the National Highways Association. This group brought forth a compendium of reasons why a nationwide highway system should be established and published a map showing where those roads should be built. The association's proposal bears a passable resemblance to the core of the U.S. highway system as it finally took form over the next two generations, before adoption of the national defense-based Interstate Highway System in 1956.

In 1916, after four years of consideration, the Congressional study report was made public and a Federal Aid Road Act was enacted. Over the succeeding four years, despite the European war which the United States joined in 1917, Congress appropriated $221 million for highway purposes, resulting in the construction of 12,919 miles of paved roads. In 1923, the first year that truly accurate statistics were compiled, Arizona — exceeded in land area by only Texas, California, Montana and New Mexico — had 1,891 miles of state highways, of which only 154 — mostly near the state capital of Phoenix — were paved. In the entire nation only 111,400 miles were paved. But even then the city of Flagstaff had paved less than a quarter mile of its downtown streets. Indeed, the later famous "Route 66" was unpaved where it passed through town, then under the name of Front Street.

On August 24, 1911, Big Red arrived in Flagstaff. Her new owner had ordered the car six months earlier and had only a few days prior just returned to his observatory from one of his frequent lecture tours. Lowell's arrival in town was soon followed by that of his newly hired chauffeur, a man who survived on the job only long enough to become known to local posterity by his first name, Louis. When Red left Arizona 28 years later, the ratio of people to automobiles in the

Opposite: Map of U.S. highway system as proposed in 1911 (Lowell Archives).

state had fallen to 3.6—not on a par with neighboring California where the ratio had gone from 27 to 2.8 over the same period, but a lot more than in Big Red's birthplace Massachusetts, which went from 57 to barely 5. In all of the United States there had been only 458,337 passenger cars registered in 1911, but when Red was to leave Flagstaff in 1938 there were more than 26 million—a more than fiftyfold increase. Nationwide, the ratio of persons to cars was 4.2. By 1938, in the entire country (not including city streets) there were now 436,731 miles of paved highways, but still extensive stretches of the Federal Highway System—particularly in the western states—remained merely graded and sometimes graveled. Despite their federal status, most of these lengthy expanses, punctuated by occasional right-angle turns at section boundaries, were muddy and dangerous in any wet weather and barely passable at all in early spring.

Total public road mileage in the country in 1938 stood at almost 3 million miles. And in the following year alone, Congress appropriated $305 million for construction of an additional 11,776 miles of paved roads—almost as much as in all the first four years of the program combined. The State of Arizona was spending $4.2 million on its own for highway construction, and registrations showed there were 136,025 total motor vehicles—686 buses, 27,349 trucks and 107,990 passenger cars. Arizona now had 2,417 miles of pavement out of the national total. The local telephone company of Flagstaff had been absorbed into the Mountain States Company of Denver and in 1926 was integrated into the nationwide Bell System. There were almost 700 phone subscribers in town. Times had very much changed!

But in some parts of the country the pollution caused by automobiles was beginning to live up to the 1896 prophecy that electric car engineer Pedro Salom, an abortive participant in Chicago's 1895 Auto Race, had published in the *Journal of the Franklin Institute*: "All the gasoline motors we have seen belch forth from their exhaust pipes a continuous stream of partially unconsumed hydrocarbons in the form of a thick smoke with a highly noxious odor. Imagine thousands of such vehicles on the streets, each offering up its column of smoke!"

Maybe the problem of the 17,000 horse cadavers removed from the streets of New York in 1890 was preferable?

X. Highways

Charles Kettering's electric starting motor made its first appearance in 1911, a year that was also notable because the saber-rattling German Kaiser Wilhelm II took the occasion in midsummer to alarm all the capitals of Europe by sending his newly-launched gunboat, *Panther,* uninvited into the harbor of Agadir on the Atlantic coast of French-dominated Morocco; the "Parliament Act" of the British House of Commons effectively emasculated the House of Lords; and on the same day the U.S. Supreme Court found John Davison Rockefeller's Standard oil Company guilty of restraint of trade. Winston Spencer Churchill left the Home Office to become First Lord of the British Admiralty; Sir William Schwenck Gilbert died, 11 years after his partner, Arthur Seymour Sullivan. Leonardo da Vinci's celebrated painting, *Mona Lisa,* was stolen from the Louvre (to be recovered two years later in Italy); Czech-Austrian composer Gustav Mahler died at age 51; Russian-born Irving Berlin, at age 23, composed his all-time favorite, "Alexander's Ragtime Band." Norwegian explorer Roald E.G. Amundsen became the first person to reach the South Pole; the demise of the Alaskan fur seal was finally halted by joint action of Japan, Great Britain, Russia and the United States; Manya Sklodowska Curie received her second Nobel Prize, this for her work in chemistry. The first 500-mile race was held at the Indianapolis Speedway (Ray Harroun's Marmon led the pack with an average speed of 74.59 MPH); on August 9, the temperature reached 100 Fahrenheit degrees in London. And on October 27, after days of rainouts, Cornelius McGillicuddy's Philadelphia Athletics beat John Joseph McGraw's New York Giants by the lopsided score of 13–2 in the sixth game, to take the World Series 4–2 and avenge the defeat of six years earlier.

Arizona was still a territory in 1911, represented in the United States Congress by 48-year-old Ralph Henry Cameron as delegate. For most of his life he was a miner and prospector, and at that time he lived in the Flagstaff area and cared about tourism and transportation, having built the Bright Angel trail down into the Grand Canyon. Like almost every other "Anglo" in the region, Cameron was an immigrant from the East, born in Southport, Maine. Though the new state was to vote Democratic in the next election, Cameron had been elected as a Republican delegate to the 61st Congress and maintained a vigorous and long-lived interest in that party. He and Big Red's owner were friends.

Arizona, organized as a territory in 1863, was finally granted statehood in the Union, effective on February 14, 1912, and Cameron, the territory's twelfth congressional delegate since organization, was replaced by 35-year-old Carl Hayden, a Democrat of Tempe who was one of the few white-skinned citizens of the new state to have actually been born there, his father having established a then-necessary ferry across the Gila River near Phoenix. Cameron (1863–1953) had opted to make a run for the Senate in Arizona's first election after statehood, but lost that time. Later, after the adoption of the Seventeenth Amendment which made senators subject to popular election, he served one full term, from 1921 to 1927.

Arizona's newly elected and now voting representative — its only member of the House — had previously been the sheriff of Maricopa County and stayed in the House of Representatives until 1927 when he was elected to the Senate, again replacing Cameron. By the time of Hayden's retirement he had served his state in Washington for a record total of 56 years and voted steadfastly for highway improvement measures on every occasion, as well as promoting the environmentally questionable bailout of real estate promoters called the Central Arizona Project.

The convoluted political history of Arizona's initial participation in the United States Congress shows a number of what would best be described a century later as labyrinthian permutations. By act of Congress on February 24, 1863, the Territory of Arizona was set off from the Territory of New Mexico and given the right to its own non-voting delegate to the 38th U.S. Congress. The person so elected was Charles Debrille Poston (1825–1902) a native of Kentucky, a Republican, and a resident of Tubac, a no longer extant locality near Florence. He was succeeded by John Noble Goodwin (1824–1887), who had previously been a representative from Maine in the 37th Congress, but, failing of re-election down east in the fall of 1862, had been appointed by President Lincoln as Chief Justice and then governor of Arizona. He served only in the 39th Congress and then left for California.

Coles Bashford (1816–1878), originally of Cold Spring, New York, and latterly of Tucson, served as an Independent delegate only

X. Highways

in the 40th Congress. He had previously been elected as governor of Wisconsin and then, upon moving again farther west, had brought that state's legal framework and precedents to Arizona as the territory's first attorney general. After his congressional stint, he became Arizona's Secretary of State for eight years. He was succeeded by Richard Cunningham McCormick (1832–1901) who had been born in New York City, been a correspondent on the scene during the Crimean War, then been appointed territorial governor by President Johnson in 1866. As another resident of Tucson, he was elected as a Unionist delegate to the 41st, 42nd, and 43rd Congresses (March 4, 1869–March 3, 1875) but declined renomination in favor of a series of prominent federal appointments, including two foreign ministries. McCormick's last political hurrah, however, saw him back in the 54th Congress as a representative from New York.

Hiram Sanford Stevens (1832–1893), a native of Weston, Vermont, had been in the U.S. military as a dragoon in the Apache Wars of 1852 and 1854, and then located as a businessman in Tucson. A Democrat, he was elected to the 44th and 45th Congresses, but lost a reelection bid in the fall of 1878. His successor, but for only the 46th Congress (March 4, 1879–March 3, 1881) was the Glaswegian John Goulder Campbell (1827–1903) who had emigrated to New York at age 14 and then gone to California as a Forty-Niner. Failing to strike it rich, he then migrated to the Prescott area, where he was first elected a territorial representative and then supervisor of Yavapai County.

Granville Henderson Oury (1825–1891), a native of Abingdon, Virginia, and a lawyer by training, had also been an unsuccessful Forty-Niner. Returning eastward to Tucson, he engaged in the practice of law as both an attorney and a judge before his election to the Confederate Congress, where he took his seat in Montgomery, Alabama, on January 21, 1862. Within months he resigned that office to serve in the Confederate Army until Texas was overwhelmed at the end of 1864. Never having taken and violated an oath of allegiance to the United States, he was allowed to take such an oath on October 8, 1865, and resumed his political involvement as a representative to the Territorial Legislature and attorney general. An unsuccessful candidate for election to the 46th Congress, he made it to the 47th and 48th, but declined reelection in the fall of 1884.

Curtis Coe Bean (1828–1904), born in Tamworth, New Hampshire, a scion of the omnipresent Bean family, was the first formally college-educated delegate elected from Arizona. Having migrated to Tennessee, he served in that state's legislature in 1867-68 and then moved west to Prescott to try his hand at mining. An unsuccessful candidate for the 45th Congress, he made it to the Territorial Senate in 1879 and was elected to the 49th Congress, but was not re-elected in the fall of 1886. Thereafter he returned to the East though maintaining his business interests in Arizona. The man who defeated him was Marcus Aurelius Smith (1851–1924), who had been born in Cynthiana, Kentucky, and served as prosecuting attorney for the city of Lexington. He went west in 1879, working as a lawyer in San Francisco, and then to Tombstone in 1882, where he again served as prosecuting attorney. Smith was elected as a Democrat to the 50th and the three succeeding Congresses, as well as to the 55th, the 57th, the 59th and the 60th. Upon the admission of Arizona to statehood, he was elected to the United States Senate for the term ending on March 3, 1915, and re-elected for the next term, after which he was appointed to the International Boundary Commission (with Canada).

Representing Arizona in the 54th Congress (March 4, 1895–March 3, 1897) was Nathan Oakes Murphy, a native of Jefferson, Maine, who had taught school in Wisconsin before settling in Phoenix, where he was appointed — as a Republican — to be governor in 1892. Declining renomination in favor of a second appointment as governor which lasted until 1902, Murphy tried again for election to the 57th Congress in 1900, but Smith was too much for him.

Two years later saw the territory represented by John Frank Wilson (1846–1911), a native of Pulaski, Tennessee, who had also served in the Confederate Army and then been elected to the Alabama legislature in 1877. Moving to Prescott in 1887, he was a member of the Territorial Constitutional Convention of 1891, held various public and political offices and finally was elected delegate to the 56th Congress in the fall of 1898. A Democrat, he alternated the Congressional office with Smith, being elected to the 58th Congress, but declining renomination both in 1900 and again in 1904.

X. Highways

Hayden's election came with that of T. Woodrow Wilson as president with less than 42 percent of the nation's popular vote, one of the lowest percentage political victories in American history, thanks to the Republican-leaning majority of the electorate being split between those loyal to incumbent William Howard Taft and those who followed his now Progressive predecessor, Theodore Roosevelt. However, in making his fourth run for the presidency, the 56-year-old Socialist from Indiana, Eugene Victor Debs, running on a platform that would qualify as conservative if not reactionary before the end of the century, had taken a respectable part of the popular vote. While he garnered more than 900,000 votes, he only carried a dozen counties nationwide, mostly in Minnesota.

While Lowell's car was en route by train to its future home in Flagstaff, one could read in the Coconino *Weekly Sun*, the town's only newspaper's edition of August 18, 1911[*]:

NORTHERN ARIZONA AND THE AUTO HIGH LINE

The Great Center of Attraction Is in This Section and the Prospect Looks Good

The following despatch comes from Prescott under recent date, and shows what is being done in the effort to establish the transcontinental automobile high line in northern Arizona. Of course the natural attractions are here and speak for themselves, but it will take some effort and some energy to establish the line through this section.

The despatch says: "Northern Arizona counties are working tooth and nail for a chain of automobile roads from Gallup, New Mexico, to the western boundary of the territory, to open up to California and eastern auto tourists, the varied charms of the Painted Desert, Petrified Forest, Moqui villages, and the Grand and Cataract Canyons.

Tom Norris, president of the Arizona Good Roads Association, [a long-lived group, whose chairmanship was later held by Earl C. Slipher of Lowell Observatory] returned from the meeting of the Arizona Good Roads Association meeting in Phoenix today. He is at present working strenuously to make a perfect success of the meeting of the territorial association in this city beginning September 2, as the Bankers

---

[*]*In the days of hand-set type, there were numerous "typos" in the daily press of all nations and cities. In the quotations used in this book, we have corrected them for ease of reading.*

Association of Arizona will convene in Prescott on the same date, and there is much to do....

Mr. Norris is planning for the publication of an Arizona Good Roads Handbook, which shall portray all the auto roads in the territory, showing small photographs of all turns, forks and cross-roads on the several roads. The book will also contain exhaustive particulars as to hotels, accommodations, watering stations and other necessary details for the comfort and convenience of the tourist. Each road will be mapped in colors and opposite each junction or cross-road point, a photograph will be inserted to prevent any possible confusion....

The Navajo and Apache county supervisors are working in harmony for the improvement of their roads to the Coconino county line and David Babbitt of Flagstaff promises the co-operation of the Coconino board to the end...."

The "Good Roads" movement was gathering momentum nationwide. One might use the phrase "gathering steam" in view of the continuing popularity of steam-powered vehicles in those days throughout the land. The very week that Percival Lowell's "explosion" engined car was delivered to Flagstaff, the *Coconino Sun* of Friday, August 18, reported that:

> The contract for the erection of the bridge across the Little Colorado river has been approved by the department [of Public Works], and that the work would be ordered to commence at a very early date. The construction of the bridge across the Little Colorado will be of untold value to this section of Northern Arizona and the beginning of work on the same will be much appreciated by the people of this section.

And two months later, on October 6, the same paper also reported that "the Fourth International Good Roads Congress, which has been in session at Chicago this week, has passed a resolution unanimously endorsing a Transcontinental Highway across the United States from New York City to Los Angeles. The proposed road, if constructed, will pass through northern Arizona." A few years later, this plan was partially realized in the laying out of the famous "Route 66."

The weekly newspaper of Flagstaff also carried regular advertisements for local business firms, some of them auto-related. In those days, the difference between a paid ad and a favorable news

X. Highways

column mention was less distinct than the later custom, but some were quite obvious. Despite the regular quarter-column ads for "O.S. (Harry) Emblem" who was "agent for Chalmers-Detroit, Pope-Hartford and Hudson automobiles" (and also did general garage work), one could learn that "Robt. Anderson" still did "General Blacksmithing, Repairing, Horseshoeing, Wagon Work" and charged "Fair Prices" for "Prompt Work." The horseless carriage had not yet put him out of business.

There were even larger ads for "The Confection Den" where there were "All Kinds of Records on Hand," and others proclaiming the virtues of owning a "Victrola or an Edison Amberola." Of greater pertinence to the automobile industry were the quarter-pages that appeared regularly on behalf of "George F. Gardiner, of Flagstaff," extolling the brilliance and wisdom of promptly buying stock in the "Northern Arizona Oil Company" which was touting the "Winslow Oil Fields" where "prospects were brighter than ever, as oil had been found in the surrounding country." Such advertisements was part of a nationwide pattern of oil field promotion, only some of which ever materialized to the benefit of those who bought the shares. Like many a "fabulous" mine in the Great American West, "salted" for the benefit of gullible Eastern or European investors, before long the Winslow Oil Fields, some 100 miles east of Flagstaff, turned out to be mostly dry wells, though in later years several bores have produced merchantable natural gas. The newspaper, since renamed as the *Arizona Sun*, continues to overlook reporting on the ultimate whereabouts of George Gardiner.

BIG RED'S CONTEMPORARIES

Percival Lowell's automobile was far from the first touring car to be made. As in many other vehicular developments, a number of European designers were in the lead.

The exact model of automobile that Percival Lowell ordered in 1910 was made by Stevens-Duryea over a four-year period after 1909 but had a number of horseless ancestors going back for a dozen years. However, the idea of enclosing a vehicle for the more comfortable transport of human beings goes back a lot farther than the evolution of the automobile. Medieval *sedan* chairs in Europe and similar, frequently enclosed, devices carried on poles for moving Chinese and Inca royalty were in use for untold hundreds of years. These used man-power in various combinations—two for most people, even the upper crust, but twelve in the case of the modern and ceremonial papal *portantina*. Thus, the various names of car body styles have an equally long ancestry. The auto style called *coupe*, for example, comes from the French word meaning *cut off* or *shortened*.

In the French-speaking countries, the auto style called *tonneau* was not translated or even transliterated into English, but duplicated as "touring car." All such vehicles had a folding roof, sometimes equipped with removable side curtains, and two banks of forward-facing seats. Most of them were designed for five persons, but some models, like Lowell's, also had an extra pair of folding seats behind

XI. Big Red's Contemporaries

the driver's bench, making them seven-passenger cars. The word *tonneau*, however, goes back a lot farther and has been translated into English as *cask, water barrel, water-cart, beer barrel* and finally *drunkard*. Percival Lowell was fluent in French — he had spent a year of his childhood attending school near Lausanne — and he would have also readily used the phrase *"Il est d'un bon tonneau,"* which translates into English as *"It is of first rate quality,"* a very fitting statement about the car he bought.

Up to the time of World War I, any passenger vehicle with greater than 50 horsepower was an expensive rarity and all those made up until 1906 were of lesser power. But, after that year, when the Spijker patents were made available to other manufacturers, almost all such vehicles, including all the large-bodied contemporaries of the Stevens-Duryea Model "Y," came with the larger and more powerful, but slower and smoother-running six-cylinder engine.

There were many manufacturers, both in Europe and America, who made touring cars. A good many of them have been discussed to greater or lesser degree in previous chapters, and the recitation that follows is meant to include the remaining possibilities that Percival Lowell had open to him when he made the decision to join the horseless crowd.

A leader among them was Louis Renault (1877–1944), who made his first automobile in the back yard of his parents' Parisian home in 1898 and, after he had made a few sales, took in his two younger brothers to establish what has become one of Europe's largest automotive firms. Unfortunately typical of a number of automotive experimenters — as in many other evolving fields of human endeavor — one of the founder's brothers, Marcel, was to die in 1903 from an accident in an automobile race. The firm's two-cylindered and two-passengered taxis made after 1906 were open for the driver but closed for the customers, and became world renowned as the means whereby the German advance was finally halted only fifty miles from Paris in September of 1914. In fact, the actual number of reserve troops brought over from Africa and then rushed from Gare Montparnasse across the city and north by road to the fluid front by General Joseph Gallieni's commandeered, 600-vehicle fleet was not all that large. But the publicity value to Renault of having had a part in stemming von Kluck's "right wing" advance was enormous. Their first six-cylinder models were produced in 1908. Later, during World War I, Renault made light tanks.

Also in France was the flamboyant financier Count Albert De Dion (1856–1946) whose name, like that of the American merchant-prince Hudson, became famous in upper crust automotive circles. Wisely, the count arranged to be blessed in his business affairs with a very competent protégé and associate, Georges Bouton (1847–1938), the son of a painter, who had designed gasoline engines for use in a variety of automobile bodies starting in 1895. In 1910, De Dion-Bouton was the first maker to come up with a successfully operable V-8 engine. Never a large-scale manufacturer like Renault, after the end of the first World War the firm gradually dwindled away, ending its days as a motorcycle maker. De Dion himself, however, was a prominent figure in popularizing the automobile, starting with the day that his powerful, steam-driven machine, with the count himself at the tiller, came in ahead of all other vehicles partaking in the 1894 Paris to Rouen race.

Still in France, the English-educated experimenter Armand Peugeot (1849–1915) made his first steam-powered cars in 1889 and then, like many of his contemporaries, graduated to use of Daimler-built internal-combustion engines in 1891. One of the most long-lived makers of automobiles in the world, the Peugeot company started making its own engines in 1896 and brought out its first six-cylinder models in 1908. In the years prior to the First World War, Peugot's racing models placed first in many events, including on one occasion and much to American embarrassment, the Indianapolis 500. In later years, Peugeot acquired the Citroen firm and much of the Chrysler Corporation's European business.

Max Cudell, a native of Aachen, was one of the pioneers of *kraft-wagen* production in Germany. His first models appeared in 1899, using De Dion engines. Making his own engines after 1904, his popular four-cylinder, tonneau models developed as much power as the later Stevens-Duryea "Big Six." Typical in his business behavior of many a competent engineer, Cudell was a constant experimenter, making various engines for his vehicles with one, two and four

XI. Big Red's Contemporaries

cylinders. The financial results of this uneconomic manufacturing process caught up with the Cudell firm in 1905, and the business was closed. Manufacturing was transferred to Berlin where the inventor's son, Paul, made a few more cars until production ceased completely in 1908.

The Searchmont touring cars were the products of a short-lived, Philadelphia-based firm, with bodies designed by Lee Sherman Chadwick (1875–1958), the Vermont-born son of a carriagemaker. The company was headed by another of those noted racing drivers who capitalized on their fame at the wheel of cars to enter the very different game of manufacturing them. Charles Fournier, scion of a family distinguished in French art, science and military history, was, however, not nearly as well-known as Louis Chevrolet, nor as well financed as other makers. Their company folded soon after developing the prototype, which most closely resembled the Stevens-Duryea Model "Y," was offered for sale at $2,500.

The Spijker brothers of Trompenberg, Netherlands, started building two-cylinder vehicles in 1900. Their name has been generally taken into English as *Spyker*, and frequently appears in the automotive literature with that spelling. The older brother, Hendrik (1855–1907), drowned at sea while returning from the East Indies and his younger brother, Jacobus (1857–1932), took over management of the business. Very innovative in its engineering, the Spijker firm was a leader in air-cooled engine and front-wheel drive design during the first quarter of the 20th century. Theirs were the first six-cylinder engines in the world, appearing in 1903. Four years later one of their cars, thus equipped, won the Peking-to-Paris endurance race. At home in the Netherlands, Spijker remains best known for having built the "golden coach" that is used for ceremonial state occasions such as coronations and the opening of parliament.

Noted mostly for their racing cars which were frequent winners in the Le Mans contests, Ernest Chenard (1861–1922) and Henri Walcker (1873–1912) first got together in 1899 to make bicycles and then began car production in the northern Paris suburb of Asnières in 1901. Their first models were unsuccessful light vehicles and the company was forced to close its doors in 1907. Relocated a short distance away to Gennevilliers and revived a few years later, the firm began a more prosperous line with sports and racing cars. Before the company was absorbed into Peugeot after World War II, it had made a complete line of automotive products from tractors to tanks, but their final models were light vans, bringing Chenard & Walcker back, unfortunately, to their origins.

Henry Ford (1863–1947), the irascible, fiercely independent-thinking son of an Irish immigrant, needs no introduction to the world. Few present-day Americans, however, are aware that his famous "Model T" was the last of an alphabetic series that began with his first Model A. Ford's Model K was a touring car and had one of America's first six-cylinder engines. But in venturing into an upscale market, Ford was momentarily out of his element and was less successful than with his immortal, but definitely plebeian, four-cylinder Model T—which stayed in production, essentially unchanged, for nineteen years after 1908. This vehicle became so much a part of American folklore that Charles Duryea wrote in the *Saturday Evening Post* in 1931, toward the end of his life, that "It may even be that the twenty-first century will think of Henry Ford as the inventor of the automobile." This author learned to drive, at the age of 13, on one of those classic vehicles, which was then much more than twice his age. And in the popular mind in the United States, Duryeas's prediction has proved essentially correct.

Benjamin Berkeley Hotchkiss (1826–1885), a Connecticut Yankee, established an arms factory at St. Denis, just north of Paris, shortly after the Franco-Prussian War of 1870, one result of which — in addition to the declaration of the German Empire at Versailles — had been the removal of much of the French prewar munitions inventory. Much as in the case of Joshua Stevens in Chicopee, this plant backed into the production of automobiles because, by 1903, the arms business was in a slump. And, again like the All-American Stevens-Duryea, the French-built Hotchkiss products were "top-of-the-line" vehicles, equipped with six-cylinder engines after 1906. Before World War I, their sports-racing cars had won the Monte Carlo rallies for five years. Their tonneaux were prized possessions of the French "Four Hundred."

Frank Ballou Stearns (1878–1955) of Cleveland was an early pioneer of automobile manufacture, starting in 1896 with a series of

XI. Big Red's Contemporaries

light cars. In 1904, however, he found his niche by following the lead of the German-built Mercedes-Benz into the high-income end of car production. His six-cylinder touring car models first appeared in 1908, with body panels made of cast aluminum, an idea cribbed from Frank Duryea. The Stearns models of that year were all individually made to order, capable of "highway" speeds in excess of 85 MPH, but bearing price tags of $6,250 and up. Percival Lowell might well have acquired one of these vehicles, had he not been a loyal Yankee at heart.

Rollin Henry White (1874–1962), also of Cleveland, first achieved financial success with his sewing machines. Then, like George Pierce and many others, he backed into car production, his first steam-powered vehicles appearing in 1900. A variety of body styles and transmission mechanisms came along until 1910, when the first gasoline "explosion" engines were offered. Steam engine production was discontinued the following year and White's sales line for the year of 1912 included a six-cylinder model. In later years, the name of White became associated mostly with heavy truck production.

The Fabbrica Italiana Automobili Torino was the 1899 brainchild of Giovanni Agnelli (1866–1945), Conte Biscaretti di Ruffia, who headed the FIAT organization until 1920, later serving as a senator. In great part because of his friendship with Benito Mussolini, Agnelli's factory became the chief war materiel producer for the unwise Italian overseas military adventures of the 1930s and then in preparation for World War II. The city of Turin, rather than the much larger neighboring metropolis of Milan, was therefore a favorite target of Allied bombers. Back in civilian work by 1946, the firm employed some of the finest car body designers available anywhere and developed numerous models that were sold all over the world. By the end of the 20th century, FIAT had become the largest employer in Italy and had manufacturing interests in many fields in two dozen countries.

The Rex-Simplex marque started out as a product of the firm of Richard & Hering, which followed a common pathway into car production. Originally makers of bicycle parts in the tiny Saxon town of Ronneburg, they started to build a line of smaller cars in 1901 powered by De Dion engines. After the end of World War I, the production of larger, luxury models was taken over by Elite, which ultimately became part of the manufacturing empire assembled by Fritz von Opel (1899–1971), grandson of the founder, Adam von Opel (1837–1895).

BEYOND LOWELL'S DEATH

Life was never the same around his observatory after Dr. Lowell died. There were many uncertainties and soon there were much younger cars on Mars Hill. The big red machine was generally forgotten in the garage under the Baronial Mansion. Finally it was decided that it should be sent away.

At age 62, Percival Lowell suffered a massive stroke on November 12, 1916, and was dead the following day. But more than any other astronomer of his age, he left a larger legacy to humanity. His dreams of Mars and the possibility of intelligent life on another world were far ahead of his peers and remain to this day the ultimate justification for taxpayer support of America's space program. His insistence on and support of V.M. Slipher's informed analysis of "spiral nebulae" led directly to our understanding of the expanding nature of the universe. His insistence that there was yet another solar system object out there beyond the planet Neptune not only led to the location of Pluto by his immediate heirs, but to the subsequent determination, mostly by those who have followed his studies on Mars Hill, of an enormous host of further "Kuiper Belt Objects" (KBOs) that lie beyond. This distant region of the solar system was named for Gerard Peter Kuiper (1905–1973), Netherlands-born American astronomer, the director of both the Yerkes and McDonald observatories, and a subsequent leading student of the sun's planetary system.

Percival Lowell at the eyepiece of his most famous telescope, the 1896 24-inch Clark refractor (Lowell Archives).

XII. Beyond Lowell's Death

As early as 1902, in a lecture at the Massachusetts Institute of Technology, where he served as an adjunct professor, Lowell had postulated the existence of yet another planet beyond the eight already identified. His prediction was based on observed irregularities in the orbit of Uranus that were not explained by the existence and "theory" of Neptune. The theory of any celestial body is based on calculations of its mass and density, coupled with analysis of all gravitational forces that act upon it. Neptune had been located in 1846 by just such analysis of inexplicable irregularities in the orbit of Uranus. However, Neptune was spotted one degree away from where the independent mathematical analyses of John Couch Adams and Urbain Leverrier had predicted. Lowell seized upon that minute discrepancy and devoted his enormous mathematical abilities to refining it, and thus determining what force could be even farther out from the sun and cause that error in his predecessors' work to exist.

Adams (1819–1892) had submitted his extensive arithmetic to the British Astronomer Royal, Sir George Airy, in 1845, suggesting it be looked for. However, that worthy simply ignored the calculations as the presumptuous scribblings of some amateur. Leverrier (1811–1871), already a distinguished French astronomer, soon performed the same exercise, but took his calculations to the more receptive Johann Gottfried Galle (1812–1910), then assistant director of the Berlin Observatory. Galle promptly spotted the new planet, on September 23, 1846, one degree away from where it had been calculated to exist. To his credit, the astronomer royal then recalled the visit of Adams and retrieved the envelope the amateur had left behind with his butler. Given the enormous distances involved and the paucity of solid data that surrounded planetary analysis in the 19th century, many astronomers were content to let the enormous arithmetical exercises of Neptune's co-discoverers rest in peace. Their separate but identical calculations were accomplishment enough. But Lowell and his Yankee contemporary and sometime employee, William Henry Pickering,* were not content. There had to be an explanation for that one degree.

---

*Both Lowell and Pickering, as well as the latter's older brother, Edward Charles, were functionaries of the Boston-based Appalachian Mountain Club, then a very scientifically oriented organization. Lowell died in office as that organization's president.

Percival Lowell's Big Red Car

After his eye-opening lecture at MIT, Lowell undertook to put his brain and his money more fully behind his prediction and engaged the services of several "computers" as he called them — mathematicians competent to handle the enormous quantity of minute data that was slowly becoming available, and reduce it to a concise analysis of what caused that one degree of discrepancy hundreds of millions of miles away from both Earth and Sun. Far different from the computers of a century later, these human beings did their work with very sophisticated slide rules and reams of paper. It was an enormous project, led by Lowell himself, but with the sustained assistance of several others. His team captain was a 1903 honors graduate of MIT, Elizabeth Langdon Williams, who worked for many years in Lowell's Boston office and then at his facility on Mars Hill, staying on even after his death and until her marriage in 1922. Finally, just a year before his death, Lowell was able to publish a detailed monograph entitled "A Trans-Neptunian Object."

To predict is one thing, but to prove is another. During the dozen years from his 1902 lecture to the publication of his monograph, Lowell had occasionally used his 24-inch refractor to scan the sky in what he felt to be the most likely areas. This telescope, now a national historic landmark, has much magnification but a correspondingly narrow field of vision, and a comparison search, such as was needed, was almost impossible with it. He then used a special 6-inch telescope made by the eminent lens and instrument maker of Pittsburgh, John Alfred Brashear (1840–1920), to test some of his conclusions, but to little practical avail. Lowell had even used his larger instrument, the 42-inch, Newtonian-focus reflector, in this process. But, with its three-times greater magnifying and light-gathering power, this instrument had an even smaller field of view. Ironically, in going back through the observatory's photographic files after the confirmed sighting of Pluto in 1930, it was discovered that Lowell had, himself, unknowingly photographed his trans–Neptunian planet a decade before his monograph was issued.

What was really needed for an effective search was an astrograph — essentially a camera with a very long telephoto lens — that could photograph a wide expanse, perhaps up to a degree, of sky and then be returned to the exact same area some days later to repeat the

XII. Beyond Lowell's Death

Percival Lowell stares out at the San Francisco peaks from his office — 1910 (Lowell Archives).

photograph. When the two plates were compared, if anything had moved in the interim between pictures it was surely much nearer to the Earth than the stars in the background that were tens and even hundreds of millions of light years away.

A light year is a prime astronomical measure of distance, along with the astronomical unit and the parsec. It is the distance that light travels in one year's time at the speed of 186,282 miles per second, and equals 5,878,000,000,000,000 miles. An astronomical unit is the average distance of the Earth from the sun: 92,560,000 miles, or somewhat less than six "light-minutes"; and a parsec, used largely for intergalactic measurements, equals 3.26 light years.

With Lowell's death and the managerial turmoil that ensued during the litigious settlement of his estate, the project of proving his calculations at Mars Hill was put on hold, though Guy Lowell did obtain the lenses suitable for a proper astrograph. Elsewhere, very few astronomers cared to risk their reputations in chasing down

Guy Lowell, the first trustee of Lowell Observatory — 1917 (Lowell Archives).

the speculations of someone who was as suspect to the professionals as that "overgrown amateur," Percival Lowell.

When the search was resumed, late in 1929 and with Guy Lowell's lenses mounted in a proper instrument, thanks to the generosity of Abbott Lawrence Lowell, Percival's one-year younger brother, it was almost immediately fruitful. Pluto, as the trans–Neptunian object was soon named by the second trustee of Lowell Observatory, was considerably smaller than Lowell's extensive arithmetic had postulated. He had anticipated finding a more Neptune-like celestial body, and this discovery was far denser than anticipated and with a more elliptical orbit. To many in the profession, confirmation of its existence only proved that there was even more out there, yet unknown and unseen. The gravitational tug which distorted the orbits of both Uranus and Neptune was due to far more than the influence of just Pluto.

By the end of the 20th century, Lowell's successors on Mars Hill had commenced the visual exploration of the vast Kuiper Belt and identified, in an ongoing program, dozens of objects that orbited the sun, but were even farther away in the outer cold. The Kuiper Belt, in turn, is less distant from the sun than the region named for another Dutch astronomer, Jan Hendrick Oort (1900–1992) who theorized in 1950 that there was a "cloud" of small objects about one light-year

XII. Beyond Lowell's Death

distant from the sun, wherein resided most comets when not visible nearer the center of the solar system.

In 1901, Percival Lowell hired a young Indiana University graduate, 26-year-old Vesto Melvin Slipher—known in all subsequent astronomical literature more simply as "V.M." As soon as he had become familiar with the Arizona surroundings—before the arrival of any newfangled automobiles on Mars Hill—V.M. expressed an interest in furthering Lowell's primary interest in the evolution of the solar system by looking closely at the cloudy surface of Venus and then at the more elusive "spiral nebulae" from the outside. At the time, it was believed that these hazy globs of light might well be other

The Slipher brothers, V.M. (left) and E.C., outside the building which now bears their family name—1948 (Lowell Archives).

solar systems in the process of formation, according to the highly publicized cosmological theories then being bruited by the English astronomer James Hopwood Jeans, and soon to be amplified in association with the much younger Harold Jeffreys. Perhaps a closer look at what was happening inside those distant and fuzzy objects might shed some light on what might have gone on a few billion years earlier in the evolution of the sun and its satellites. It could be the route to understanding the sun's own ultimate fate, and that of its planetary system.

An essential step in stellar analysis is to study the spectrum of light emanating from the object under inspection. This process can lead to a partial determination of the object's composition, for different elements exhibit different qualities and colors in the light they emit or reflect. John Brashear, who had already supplied Percival Lowell with telescopes on loan when the Mars Hill facility was first opened, was asked if he could fabricate an instrument suitable to analyze this phenomenon. Could he fabricate a spectrograph capable of analyzing the light from these spiral nebulae? When told that it would be difficult, Lowell, who spared no expense in demanding the finest equipment obtainable, asked Brashear to do his best. Slipher would have to learn how to "tame" this new instrument, much as had the distinguished William Wallace Campbell of Lick Observatory when he obtained an earlier version of such a device from Brashear in 1894. Campbell (1862–1939) was one of America's most illustrious scientists and educators, receiving international recognition as president of the University of California. However, he was also among the leading skeptics of the novel toils and disconcerting though well publicized pronouncements of Percival Lowell.

Once the spectrograph was on hand, and soon after starting his efforts, Slipher asked to be allowed to visit with Campbell and learn from the older man's experiences with the earlier spectrograph. But Lowell, who enjoyed very acrimonious relationships with most of his professional peers in the field of astronomy, would hear none of it. Slipher was to do it on his own and not go near anyone such as Campbell until he had become familiar enough to "give them as much as you take." It was not an easy prohibition, but Slipher did his best. He began by studying the spectra of light reflected from the big outer

XII. Beyond Lowell's Death

planets, resulting before long in learning that in some of the bands in their spectra there was a high rate of absorption at the red end. Though Slipher refused to speculate on what this meant, later astronomers were able to determine that this phenomenon indicated the presence of methane and ammonia in the planets' atmospheres.

But it was to be the more distant spiral nebulae that became Slipher's obsession and ultimate claim to major astronomical fame. When he started looking at the complete gamut of light coming from them, he noticed that almost invariably it was all shifted toward the red end of the spectrum and away from the blue. This was puzzling — why were more than 95 percent of these objects shifted one way and only a few the other, and even fewer barely shifted at all? For the ten years prior to his employer's death Slipher was almost the only scientist studying this matter, and he compiled a list of 41 of these nebulae with radial velocities ranging from 300 kilometers per second to as high as 1,800 Km/sec of recession from our sun. Though again he refused to hypothesize on the significance of his discovery — his employer had excited more than enough controversy by that sort of speculation — intense analysis of Slipher's data could come to only one conclusion. Most of these bodies, whatever their nature, were moving away from the Sun, and in some cases at frighteningly large speeds.

All subsequent scientists credit V.M. Slipher with the discovery of the "red shift" and its obvious inference that these distant galaxies, some much larger than our parent galaxy, the Milky Way, are receding from Earth. The visible universe was obviously still expanding from its initial starting point. A generation later, Edwin Powell Hubble, at Mount Wilson Observatory, took Slipher's finding one step further by determining that the more distant the galaxy, the faster it appeared to be receding, and thereby placed his name in the astronomical lexicon one Big Bang notch ahead of V.M.

The will of Percival Lowell, executed on February 21, 1913, and witnessed by several longtime associates, was clear:

> First, I appoint my wife, Constance S. Lowell, and my brother-in-law, William Lowell Putnam, executors, and desire that no bonds be required of said executors or of any administrator with the will annexed, or of any trustee under this will.

Percival Lowell's Big Red Car

William Lowell Putnam, II, with his wife, Elizabeth, favorite sister of Percival Lowell—1913 (Lowell Archives).

Second, I authorize my executors to sell any property real or personal, without leave of any court.

Third, I give to said Constance S. Lowell the sum of One Hundred and Fifty Thousand ($150,000) Dollars and all my personal and household effects *and my automobile* [emphasis added].

Fourth, all the rest and residue of my property I give to my brother-in-law, William Lowell Putnam, to be held subject to the provisions hereinafter made for my wife, in trust for the Lowell Observatory. The property shall be invested. Ten (10) percent of the net income shall be added yearly to the principal, and the balance of the net income shall be used for carrying on the study of Astronomy, and especially the study of our Solar System and its evolution, at my observatory, at Flagstaff, Arizona, and at such other places as may from time to time be convenient....

The remainder of the typed will was two pages long, single spaced and very specific. Later codicils gave Constance even more capital and half the net income from the residual estate and *"the right to live in and enjoy the B.M. house at the Lowell Observatory during her life."* But the lady was still not satisfied; by a final codicil she had been named the sole executor of her husband's will and upon his death could run everything until the estate was finally settled and turned over to the trustee. This last was a condition she turned out

XII. Beyond Lowell's Death

to be in no hurry to bring about. Aided by pragmatic advice (if not outright avarice) from her nephew and heir, Richmond Keith Kane, a native of San Francisco and Harvard graduate but on his way to becoming a prominent New York lawyer, she also evolved the idea that the will of Percival Lowell constituted "a private perpetuity," a legal concept contrary to the law in most jurisdictions. If the will could be declared invalid, then she (and her sister's offspring) would be the beneficiaries and get it all — the observatory, the car, and the whole estate. The latter had been worth close to $3 million at the time of Lowell's death, a very considerable sum in 1916.

Soon after Lowell's death the big red car brought his one-time Japanese secretary, Miyaoka Tsonejiro, to his gravesite on Mars Hill —1917 (Lowell Archives).

By a different codicil, the first trustee was supposed to be Percival's nephew, George Putnam, eldest son of his second and favorite sister, Elizabeth. But he, being newly married and just starting his career in finance and investment, promptly declined to serve. Constance's belligerence, as exhibited in a spate of telegrams from Flagstaff to Boston, was more than George needed. Lowell Observatory was thus deprived of the fiscal supervision and advice of a man whose name came to carry enormous weight in American financial circles. The will's backup clause relative to the trusteeship required that George's other maternal uncle, Lawrence, find a replacement.

While Constance engaged the legal services of Judge Doe, a popular local attorney in northern Arizona and Percival's "old friend," to contest the will in the courts of Arizona, Lawrence

Top: Judge E.M. Doe, walking to court in Prescott—1922. *Bottom:* Coconino County Court House—1895 (Lowell Archives).

enticed 46-year-old Guy Lowell, a distinguished architect, servant of the public, and cousin of Percival, to assume the position of trustee. The first person actually to serve as trustee of the Lowell Observatory was thus obligated to defend the founder's will against the legal onslaughts of his widow. The case remained open for years; Constance was in no hurry to lose her absolute power and used every delaying mechanism her counsel could devise. Sadly, at the culmination of this legal effort Guy was to be denied the able aid of William Lowell Putnam, II, Percival's brother-in-law and a noted Boston attorney, who had drawn up the will. He died on July 26, 1924, just at the moment when his wisdom, testimony and input were most needed.

Almost as debilitating as Dickens' celebrated *Bleak House* case of *Jarndyce v Jarndyce*, the unsettled condition

XII. Beyond Lowell's Death

and subsequent litigation dragged on for most of nine years. The corpus of the estate shriveled under Constance's frivolous and inexperienced management, legal bills soaked up much of the proceeds, and the observatory staff, which now had to walk a tightrope between the legally appointed trustee and their founder's executrix, was without any firm direction and frequently without pay. Finally, after almost interminable legal delays, on October 9, 1925, the Arizona Supreme Court (Justices Ross, McAlister and Lockwood) handed down a decision in the case of *Lowell v Lowell* stating definitively that there was nothing wrong with a perpetuity "in the public interest."

Thus armed, late in 1925, the first trustee was at last able to get the estate settled. Over the next year, the funds and the observatory's control were removed from the widow's capricious custody, and orderly management of the now sadly diminished residue could

Workmen assembling Percival Lowell's granite mausoleum — 1924 (Lowell Archives).

begin. In the meantime Constance had freely flitted back and forth across the country and built an impressive mausoleum of Quincy granite for her late husband. On May 7, 1919, she had even inspected the new Administration [now Slipher] Building with a view toward installing a pipe organ in its acoustically troublesome rotunda. When Guy Lowell got control, late in 1926, there was only half as much value to the estate as there had been when Percival died ten years earlier. Moreover, the lengthy legal and emotional dispute with such an assertive lady had sapped the trustee's strength; his professional livelihood had suffered as well. A few months after the final court decree became implemented, he embarked on a vacation trip to Europe, but died on February 4, 1927, while his ship was still at sea.

Guy Lowell was cognizant of the clear intent of his cousin's will, which also contained the clause, relative to the trustee of the estate and the observatory: "In selecting a successor, I hope that preference will be given to a male descendant of my immediate family if a suitable one exists." But Constance had given Percival no children (she was aged 44 at the time of her marriage) and so the term "family" came to encompass the wording of the next paragraph in the will, which made reference to a preference for the descendants "of my father, Augustus Lowell." In all, it was a good will and a strong will, making provisions for the orderly conduct of Lowell's observatory for all time. Now, with only occasional lingering resentments and harassments on the part of the long-lived widow (Constance's funeral was held on September 27, 1954, almost 38 years after that of her husband.) and her shrewdly artful nephew and heir, Lowell Observatory could resume its work as its founder had wished.

Constance rarely drove the car she had inherited. While impressive, it is not an easy vehicle to maneuver and she may well have been slightly afraid of it. During her lengthy absences from the observatory, Big Red was largely unused, wasting away in the garage under the final extension at the westerly end of Lowell's rambling, wooden house on Mars Hill. But Carl Lampland noted under date of Sunday, May 11, 1919, that U.S. Senator Henry Fountain Ashurst was in town to visit the observatory. He was kept busy nearly all day driving the auto for Mrs. Lowell's special guest wherever that dignitary wished to travel. Ashurst was pretty much of a local boy, though born in

XII. Beyond Lowell's Death

Winnemucca, Nevada. A Democrat by political persuasion, he had been speaker of the lower house in the territorial legislature, then district attorney of Coconino County for several years prior to 1908 and, by one of the first acts of the new state's legislature, was unanimously elected to the office of United States senator. Reelected in 1916 to a six-year term after the adoption of the 17th Amendment, he was returned by the people in 1922, 1928 and 1934.

Big Red was normally garaged under the northwest corner of Lowell's "Baronial Mansion," a rambling structure that had started out in 1894 as a two-room "warming hut" for observers' use. Over the years it had been added to in all directions as the founder took up permanent residence and his numerous guests and staff had need for housing. The final addition had been built six weeks before the arrival of the automobile and included special quarters for both the vehicle and its chauffeur. But the car tended to scare people with its occasional malfunctions. Toward the end of October in 1919, its carburetor caught fire as Lampland was returning Mrs. Lowell from a

V.M. Slipher's Hupmobile crossing the Little Colorado River, just above the Grand Falls. Big Red had enough clearance to make it unassisted — 1915 (Lowell Archives).

Percival Lowell's Big Red Car

trip to the bank downtown. The question of its danger to the observatory as a fire hazard was avoided a month later when it was driven to Los Angeles, where it languished for the next six years, Mrs. Lowell being too preoccupied with other matters to care about paying for its repair and then returning it to home. Finally, late on the afternoon of September 27, 1925, Constance returned from Los Angeles, driven the whole distance by Guy Sykes.

The big red car continued to perform tolerably and was used to take various visitors on a number of outings around the region, to the Grand Canyon and Meteor Crater, for example. On his first visit to the observatory after becoming its trustee, in May of 1927, Roger Putnam, with his wife and sister-in-law, drove as far afield as the Montezuma Well. Lampland had gotten its foibles tolerably well in

Carl Lampland taking members of the V.M. Slipher family out for a spin in Big Red —1912 (Lowell Archives).

XII. Beyond Lowell's Death

hand and Stanley Sykes's periodic ministrations with the help of his sons, Harold and Guy, kept it roadworthy. It was even driven back to Los Angeles early in 1928 for a paint job. But after Guy brought it back from the Coast, the car was largely unused and immobile. Its aging rubber tires began to crack and then went flat.

The offices and library of the observatory were in a classic, stone-faced structure constructed in 1915–16 from plans that had been drawn up earlier by Guy Lowell under commission from Percival. This building was separated from the garage under Lowell's "Baronial Mansion" by only a few feet. As with most cars of that vintage, and some even much younger, there were drips from the crankcase and minor leaks from the gasoline lines, which continually combined to create fumes of a potentially incendiary, if not explosive, nature.

The newly installed director (he had been "acting" for the previous ten years), the increasingly distinguished V.M. Slipher, was concerned that an electrical malfunction in the primitive wiring of the old house might set things off. Actual ownership of the ramshackle building was somewhat in doubt, as Constance had been given lifetime rights of occupancy, but refused to pay for any maintenance or repair. As a result the building also degenerated and its disrepair could be readily seen just a few yards from the director's office window at the east end of the observatory's new administration building. Slipher alleviated his growing concerns by boarding in the open porches adjacent to his office and complaining with increasing vigor to the observatory's trustee, now Percival's nephew, Roger Lowell Putnam, who had been named to the position of trustee in the will of Guy Lowell. This was George Putnam's brother, the second son of Percival's sister, Elizabeth, and also figured prominently in the business and political life of Massachusetts.

At certain times of the year Arizona's forests become particularly susceptible to fire. By virtue of an act of Congress on May 30, 1910, "section numbered seventeen, in township numbered twenty-one north of range seven east of the Gila and Salt River base meridian," having been deeded to Percival Lowell, his corporate heirs and assigns "for observatory purposes," the observatory now owned considerably more than a square mile of forested land, mostly to the west. This was good for protection against excessive light pollution and unwanted encroachment, but it also caused concern because of the frequent presence of unknown and transient trespassers. After one of his periodic visits, under date of May 25, 1938, the trustee, now also the mayor of Springfield, wrote in his customary gentle style to urge that something had to be done about this threat.

V.M. Slipher (left) and Stanley Sykes hang a wreath on Lowell's mausoleum in 1955 — the centennial of his birth. (Lowell Archives).

We didn't go terribly far on the fire situation, but I do hope you can find ways of removing the garage and the red car to help that hazard. It is at this time of year that I worry most.

I wonder, too, if it would not be a good idea, during the dry months, to make it a point to have some one of the staff on duty as "officer of the day," particularly on Saturdays, Sundays and holidays. I should suppose that this could be done without serious hardship, because the schedule need not be iron-clad, and people can sway their dates around if they conflict with picnics or other family affairs....

Coincidentally, on the very next day, "V.M." had started a two-page, six-point letter to the trustee, back at the Package Machinery Company offices in Springfield:

> 5, The City has promised to give us a new water line, and I presume the work can be done in the near future. This will make us feel much safer. [Over the years the water storage on Mars Hill had steadily increased. The original stone tank built by Dr. Lowell holds 10,000 gallons; a replacement built in 1950 holds 30,000 and an additional tank in 1994 holds 150,000 gallons.]
> The improvement of the drive to the Observatory is something that is so much a public need that we can urge it strongly and if need be

XII. Beyond Lowell's Death

bring pressure sufficient to ensure the work will be done this summer. I am glad you wrote Mr. Walkup of the County Board of Supervisors and to Mayor Saunders, for you urged these matters in a nice way and faced them with a written demand for improvements that are and have long been needed.

6, Mrs. Lowell expressed willingness to consider disposing of the Red Car, and I promised her to have Mr. Sykes's son look it over and to tell her what he thought the best way to market it. He is expected here soon and then we can get in touch with Mrs. Lowell again. With the Car out of the picture we then can I think hope to get Mrs. Lowell's consent to taking the garage down in sections and moving it away to another site, and this will be quite a help in separating the buildings a bit. Your letter has come since I started this to you. We generally have had a summer schedule and another has been put into effect, for we have always wanted some one here at all times, and I am glad to have your suggestion.

As the issue was worked out over the summer, it became clear that either Constance, who had lifetime rights of tenancy in the house and also owned the car, would have to keep Big Red in better repair, or the increasingly venerable, but now increasingly tired, machine would have to leave Mars Hill. It was a sad but necessary ultimatum and Constance ended up taking the easy way out.

Henry Lee Giclas, whose father had helped construct parts of the Mars Hill facility and whose entire working career was spent in association with Lowell Observatory, later took up that final part of Big Red's saga on Mars Hill:

> About 1938 Mrs. Lowell gave the 1911 red Stevens-Duryea touring car to Mr. T. Paul Dalzell, part-owner and manager of the Puritan Ice and Storage Company of Santa Barbara, California, for use in the annual Fiesta Parade of that city. Mrs. Lowell, V.M. Slipher and Carl Lampland were stockholders of the Storage Company, an investment Mrs. Lowell got into on one of her visits to California. Stanley Sykes, his son, Harold, and I had to prepare this venerable old car for its last trip in Flagstaff. By then all the tires were flat and the inner tubes rotted. It was impossible to buy tubes for the tires anywhere around town, as they were 3½ inches by 36 inches in diameter. We had to have motorcycle tubes vulcanized together to make the replacement tubes. Stanley and Harold, with a little help from others of us, got the automobile running in fine shape, but then Lampland, who had driven it for many

Percival Lowell's Big Red Car

Top: Stanley Sykes (left) surveys the decrepit condition of Big Red before her last trip down Mars Hill—1938. *Bottom:* Big Red starts on her "final" trip down Mars Hill; Harold Sykes is at the wheel—1938 (Lowell Archives).

XII. Beyond Lowell's Death

years while Percival Lowell was alive, wanted to take it for the final spin. Stanley and Harold were very much opposed because they feared Lampland would try to "hot rod" it and all their work of the past week would go for naught. But the sturdy old vehicle withstood that final test and the next day, with Mrs. Lowell sitting in the extra-wide back seat that had been constructed for her comfort, her black veil trailing in the wind, the car was driven down Mars Hill for the last time and into a waiting box car on the siding by the old freight depot. I took some 8mm movies of that last drive, but had to hide behind a tree because Mrs. Lowell did not want her picture taken.

There are a few addenda to this story. Some years later I told Mrs. Lowell how we hated to see the old car leave Flagstaff, and how nice it would have been to drive it in the University's Homecoming Parades. To this she replied, "Well, why didn't you ask me for it?" Of course, that was easy for her to say then as I do not believe she would have left it with us in any case. Years later, to add insult to injury, some antique dealer from California wrote to the Observatory asking if we would like to buy it back for a bargain price of $50,000. Very soon after Mrs. Lowell returned to Boston, to everyone's relief, V.M. had the offending garage torn down so as to have adequate space for fire protection between the decrepit, rambling, wooden building and the Observatory's administration headquarters.

The final word appeared in the *Coconino Sun* of 16 September, 1938:

Mrs. Constance E. Lowell yesterday shipped from Lowell Observatory here the 1911 custom-built Stevens-Duryea automobile that she and the late Dr. Percival Lowell once used, to P.T. Dalzell of Santa Barbara, California. Last week Mrs. Lowell shipped two carriages, a phaeton and a runabout, to Mr. Dalzell, who plans to give the three vehicles a comfortable home on his ranch and use them in pageants on the Coast. The old automobile was the red car, well known to residents of Flagstaff many years ago. It was last used in 1927, bearing license plates of that year. The car has six cylinders, one of the very few so powered. The engine is extremely long; each cylinder has two spark plugs, fired by both ignition of battery and magneto. Carbide lamps have been transformed to electric but otherwise the car appears the same as when it was specially built at Chicopee Falls, Massachusetts. Plenty of brass ornaments ... and the upholstery is of leather of a high quality rarely seen now.

Big Red was gone, everyone assumed, forever.

BIG RED COMES HOME

It was sixty years before the big red car was truly back on Mars Hill. In the meantime, the fifth owner had brought it to Flagstaff, at first without knowing it was home. Then it participated in some Arizona road rallies with the observatory's fourth trustee as navigator. Later, at the request of the trustee, Mr. Eastwood brought it to the observatory for the centennial party in 1994 and advised the trustee that if he was going to build any new structures on Mars Hill, he should make provision for a large garage stall.

Warwick Eastwood, who died in January 2002, as this book was being prepared, was another English-born engineer, like Stanley Sykes, and he even worked in an area similar to an observatory. He and his twin brother, Douglas, could have been reincarnations of Stanley Sykes and his older brother, Godfrey, who had helped build Lowell's observatory a hundred years earlier. Warwick, always called "Woody," worked for the Jet Propulsion Laboratory in Pasadena, where he made the fine elements needed for intricate moving parts and electronic devices that had to be reliable when rocketed hundreds of millions of miles into space — a long way from any repair garage.

Big Red came back to Flagstaff in June of 1989, towed on a trailer behind Woody's heavy, black Cadillac. The Horseless Carriage Club of America had organized a "Big Car" tour in Northern Arizona and

XIII. Big Red Comes Home

Top: Warwick Eastwood (Woody) pauses at work making a replacement part —1995 (M. Eastwood). *Right:* Big Red held an appropriate California vanity plate while owned by Warwick Eastwood —1996.

more than 100 pre–1916 vintage vehicles were roaming the streets and roads of the area. As a part of the tour, many historic locations in Flagstaff were visited and the car was driven back up to the observatory on Mars Hill. The parade of old cars had stopped on the paved circle outside the observatory's Slipher Administration Building. Dr. Henry Giclas, now retired but still very active in

Percival Lowell's Big Red Car

observatory affairs, had helped to prepare Big Red half a century earlier for its final trip down the hill to be shipped away to Santa Barbara. When he looked out his office window at the lineup of old cars, he commented to one of his younger associates that "One of them looks remarkably like Dr. Lowell's car."

On the last day of the tour, Douglas Eastwood, Woody's twin brother and one of the participants visited the Pioneer Museum, on the north edge of Flagstaff, with his wife and happened to see in a display case the 1915 registration card of a Stevens-Duryea car. He made a note of the vehicle number and took it outside to his brother, to ask if the car still existed, Woody being the "official keeper" of the Stevens-Duryea registry, knew there were only about 100 vehicles of that make still in operation, out of some 15,000 that had been manufactured. Woody took one look at the paper that his brother handed him showing number 20700 and assured him that the car not only existed, but "it's right over there in the parking lot." Warwick Eastwood was driving around Flagstaff in Percival Lowell's "Big Six"— its fifth owner!

Having returned to the museum to verify the accuracy of his brother's note-taking, Woody thereupon drove Big Red back up to Mars Hill for a joyful "photo op" with members of the observatory staff, of whom only the octogenarian Giclas had personal knowledge of the vintage vehicle. While the joyful, yet tearful, reunion was in progress, everyone on the scene "knew" in his heart that the old car had come "home." Woody was kind enough to bring it back on several further occasions until finally he made what this writer called a "sweetheart" offer, which was promptly accepted. The old car cost its newest owner more than twenty times what it had cost its first owner, but considering three generations of inflation and resultant scarcity, it was a steal!

Warwick Eastwood grins as he returns custody of Big Red to Lowell Observatory—1999.

XIII. Big Red Comes Home

On March 1, 2000, Warwick Eastwood, octogenarian auto buff and the 1959 president of the Horseless Carriage Club of America, told how he had come by the big red car.

On May 7th of 1970 I bought Big Red from Adolph Whitney. He was a dairy farmer who lived at 6613 Riverside Drive in Pasadena but had developed heart problems and didn't want to keep the car up any longer. I figured it would fit right in with my 1905 Buicks and an earlier Stevens-Duryea, so I bought it. I guess Uncle Percy paid about $6,000 for the car, perhaps a little more because of the extra body work to make that rear seat wider; I paid a lot more. You know, I've appointed myself official keeper of the Stevens-Duryea register. There's only about a hundred of these wonderful cars left in the whole world, but the Model "Y" was the cream of the crop. This car was designed in 1908 and offered for sale in 1909, 1910, 1911 and 1912. Model "Y" was available in two wheel bases and in five passenger and seven passenger styles. At the end of 1912 models "Y," "X" and the model "AA" "Light Six" were discontinued and replaced with the six cylinder Model "C."

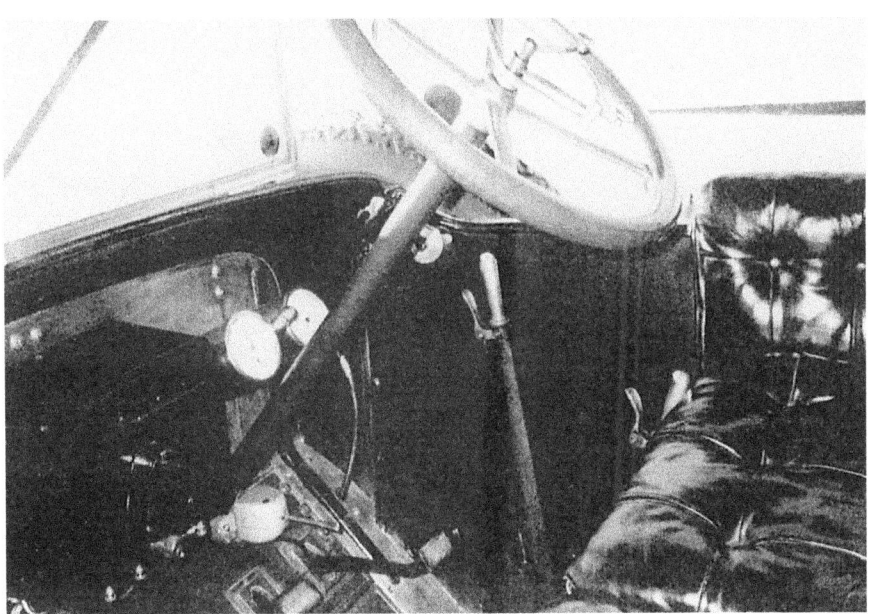

Interior control panel

Percival Lowell's Big Red Car

This car's odometer said it only had 1775 miles on it when I purchased it. Because I've found the odometer gear tends to become loose and not register after a spell on bumpy roads, it may not have always been recording the car's travel, so I'm quite sure that was not really the truth, but it certainly looked like it had never been mistreated.

Car frame 20700, engine 623, was purchased by Lindley Bothwell, an antique dealer, in 1940 from Donald P. Dalzell, of Santa Barbara, son of the man who had acquired it from Mrs. Constance Lowell. Paul Dalzell was ill and finally died in 1947; meanwhile the car was no longer wanted by the family. Prior to 1938, when Mrs. Lowell disposed of it, the car had only a few mechanical changes. The head lamps had been electrified, a chain drive Wagner electric starter was installed, along with an electric generator. The fan had to be changed to a different type in order to give clearance for the radiator at the starter drive sprocket on the front of the crank shaft. The original wheels had been replaced with Baker demountable split-rim wheels which may have been removed from a large Buick. In 1945 Bothwell had the car repainted almost the same as the original color, and a new canvas top cover was made.

Big Red decorated for its Rose Bowl appearance by a team of Dutch florists — 1993 (M. Eastwood).

XIII. Big Red Comes Home

Bothwell sold the car to Whitney in 1948. The car was driven by Whitney in the 1950 Horseless Carriage Club of America National Tour from Los Angeles all the way to San Francisco. But after 1952 it was in storage on blocks most of the time until Whitney sold it to me.

Once I got it back into its original form I was very proud of owning such a fine machine and did not hesitate to show it off. The Rose Bowl Committee, a big deal here in Pasadena, got wind of it and in 1993, its 101st year, I was invited to take Angela Lansbury — the Rose Bowl Grand Marshal that year — as a passenger in the Tournament of Roses Parade and then drive the old car right out onto the field for the coin toss at the start of the game. That was a good game — Washington State vs. Michigan — but those bad Wolverine guys from the Big Ten beat our Pac Ten Huskies in a one touchdown squeaker. In that respect it wasn't as good a game as the year before, when the Huskies tromped all over the Wolverines.

The old car sometimes runs a little hot when she's driven slowly in low gear, like in a parade, but we managed to make it OK. You'll find that at the altitude of Flagstaff she'll run hot almost all the time, except

Big Red in Pasadena's Rose Bowl, Woody at the wheel — 1993 (M. Eastwood).

on really cold days. The cooling water boils at only about 170° there and that thinner air doesn't give as much cooling in its passage through the radiator. I've always carried a few extra gallons of water when I've gone to visit you.

Though the Santa Fe railroad was still very much in business—running upwards of a hundred trains a day through the center of town—this return was unlike Big Red's first arrival in Flagstaff. The car traveled from west to east and by highway. Encased in a well-insured specialty moving van, Red made the trip "via the Interstate."

Once Big Red was home to stay, in the late summer of 1999 its sixth owner drove the car down to the annual Pioneer's Picnic of the Arizona Historical Society. There, its 1915 Arizona registration, bearing #1871, was reunited with the car that now bore Arizona license plate "Horseless Carriage 13." A crowd of 250 people witnessed the reunion and the present author, Lowell Observatory's fourth trustee, made the following speech:

Earl Slipher, Jr. looks over Warwick Eastwood's three prized 1905 Buicks—1995 (M. Eastwood)

XIII. Big Red Comes Home

Big Red stares from her latest garage on Mars Hill. Note odometer attachment to right front wheel — 2000.

It was with great pleasure that I was able to arrange the reacquisition of Percival Lowell's big, red touring car earlier this year. Many people in Flagstaff have glimpsed it in recent years, when its most recent owner, Warwick Eastwood, was kind enough to bring it here for special occasions. A very few others may recall the car when it was actually in use on the streets of Flagstaff by Dr. Lowell — often by his chauffeur, Gormley; and more latterly by a staff astronomer, Dr. Carl Otto Lampland. It is my intention to donate the car to the observatory and for the observatory, in turn, to make it available on appropriate occasions in and for the city of Flagstaff and within the State of Arizona — after all, the car is older than the state. In the meantime, those who would like to arrange for its attendance at some function should do business with Earl Slipher or me, personally.

The Duryea brothers were the original automobile makers of North America, testing their newfangled horseless carriages on the streets of Springfield, Massachusetts, the city where I was born. This 1911 Stevens-Duryea was made in the neighboring community of Chicopee Falls, to the special order of my great-uncle. It arrived in Flagstaff by

Percival Lowell's Big Red Car

Big Red today, at Lowell Observatory.

rail and lived on Mars Hill until 1938, when it was transferred to a friend by my great uncle's widow, Constance. But it has always truly belonged here and I am very proud to have been able to bring it back.

The car is in mint condition, as good — maybe even better than — the day it arrived, close to ninety years ago. It was rehabilitated to its original specifications by the personal efforts of Mr. Eastwood — to whom, we — and the entire community — owe great thanks for his generous and loving care of our museum piece. However, I must tell you that I would not have had the courage to reacquire this venerable vehicle if I had not been assured of having the ongoing help of Earl Slipher, Jr. in providing it with tender, loving care. Not only did he know and enjoy this car in his childhood on Mars Hill, but he went on to become one of this community's better names in car care.

The Stevens-Duryea Company is now long gone, though my wife has memories of bridge-playing with Mrs. Frank Duryea, widow of the company's founding genius. In its day, the company was one of the premier automobile makers of the world, and, many times in my youth,

XIII. Big Red Comes Home

I went by the factory building where this car had been produced. Even that building is now gone, however — a victim of urban renewal. But having this car back on Mars Hill assures it of replacement parts if ever needed, for I believe that the machine shop which can turn out the intricate parts needed for our telescopes can also make pistons, leafs and wheels.

INDEX

Adams, J.C. 143
Adams, H.U. (Grizzly) 50
Agnelli, G. 139
Airy, Sir G. 143
Arizona Territory 123, 128; delegates to Congress 128–130
Ashurst, Hon H.F. 154
autos, landmark dates of 22, 155

Babbitt, The Hon B. 4
Barnum, P.T. 22
Benz, K. 21, 30
Blanchard, T. 14–19; steamboats of 19
Brashear, J. 144, 148
Brayton, G.B. 24
Boston & Albany Railroad 85, 88
Boston & Maine Railroad 85, 87, 88

Cameron, The Hon R.H. 127
Campbell, Dr. W.W. 148
Chadwick, L.S. 137
Chenard, E. 137
Chevrolet, L. 68, 137
Chicago "Race" 50–54
Chicago *Times/Herald* 50
Chicopee (Massachusetts) 84, 111
Chrysler, W. P. 65
Clapp, H.W. 41

Cline, Dr. P. 4
Coconino *Sun:* advertisements in 133; quotes from 77, 89, 95–97, 131, 132, 161
Cudell, M. 136
Cugnot, N. 18, 20

Daimler, G. 21
De Dion, A. 136
Denver & Rio Grande Railroad 90
Dodge Bros. (H.E. & J.F.) 67
Doe, Hon, E.M. 152
Douglass, A.E. 4, 10, 93
Durant, W.C. 67
Duryea, C.E. 28–32; death of 32; family of 31
Duryea brothers 19; ancestry of 29; first cars of 40

Eastwood, W. 162, 163, 164, 165

FIAT (Fabbrica Italiana Automobili Torino) 139
Ford, H. 138
Flagstaff (Arizona) 7, 92, 99, 116, 122

Galle, J.G. 143
Gillett, Hon, F.H. 123

173

Index

Goodrich, Dr. B.F. 71
Goodyear, C. 70
Grand Falls (Little Colorado River) 96

Hewitt, G.H. 41
highways, U.S. 119–126, 131, 132
Hotchkiss, B.B. 138
Howe, W. 85
Hudson, J.L. 27

Kane R.K. 151
Kettering, C.F. 61, 127
Knox, H.A. 34–36
Kohlsaat, H.H. 50
Kuiper, G. 141

Lampland, C.O. 79, 98, 107–108, 113–116, 117
Lee, Col. R. 16
Lenoir, J.E. 21
Leonard, W.L. 3, 79, 80, 116
Leverrier, U. 143
Lockheed, M. & A.H. 71
Lowell Dr. A.L. 4, 74, 146
Lowell, Amy 73
Lowell, Augustus 72
Lowell, Elizabeth 4, 73, 150
Lowell, Guy 146, 154, 157
Lowell, Katherine 4
Lowell, Percival: automobile of 12, 107, 111, 113, 117, 154–157, 159–161, 162–171; biographies of 3; early life of 100–101; grave 153; pictures of ii, 2, 8, 11, 76, 79, 100, 102, 104, 142, 145; siblings of 4, 72–75, 146, 150; "A Trans-Neptunian Object" (monograph) 144; will of 149–150, 153

MacArthur, A. 84
Mack, J.M. & Bros. 69
Marcus, S. 21
Mars Hill 121, 151

New York Times, quote from 32
Newcomen, T. 18

Olds, R.E. 60
Olley, M. 38
Oort, J.H. 146, 147
Opel, A. von 140
Otto, N. 21
Overman, A.H. 33

Packard, J.W. 64
Peugeot, A. 146
Pickering, W.H. 143
Pluto, search for 103–105, 141, 143–146
Putnam, G. 151
Putnam, R.L. 118, 157–158
Putnam, W.L., II 150
Putnam, Mrs. W.L. 4, 150

"Red Shift" 149
Remington, W. 41
Renault, L. 135
Rex-Simplex (automobile) 139
Rolls, C.S. 36
Rolls-Royce Company 36–39
Royce, Sir F.H. 36

Salom, P. 126
Sandow, E. 95
Santa Fe Railroad 8, 89–92
Schiaparelli, V. 101, 110
Slipher, E.C., Jr. 100, 147, 171
Slipher, V.M. 79, 103, 104, 141, 147, 148, 149, 157–158
Springfield (Massachusetts) 13
Springfield Armory 13–19
Springfield *Republican* 17
Springfield *Shopping News* 18
Spyker Bros. 137
Stanhope (Earl of Chesterfield) 42
Stanley F.E. 63–64
Stanley, F.O. 63–64
Stearns, F.B. 138
Stevens, J. 32–33; Arms & Tool Company 42–43
Stevens-Duryea models 43–49; promotions for 55–58, 81–82
Stone, A. 85
Strauss, Dr. D. 3

Index

Studebaker, C. 65
Stutz, H.C. 69
Sykes, G. 4, 9
Sykes, S. 9, 10, 108, 116, 159, 160

Tombaugh, Clyde 104
Trevithick, R. 20

Walcker, H. 137
Washington, George 13–14
Waters, A. 15
White, A.W. 52
White, R.H. 139
Williams (Arizona) 78
Williams, E.L. 144

www.ingramcontent.com/pod-product-compliance
Ingram Content Group UK Ltd.
Pitfield, Milton Keynes, MK11 3LW, UK
UKHW042015140426
5217IPUK00015B/1191